THE
DOUGH CRAFT
SOURCEBOOK

THE DOUGH CRAFT SOURCEBOOK

50 ORIGINAL PROJECTS TO BUILD YOUR MODELLING SKILLS

SOPHIE-JANE TILLEY AND SUSAN WELBY

HAMLYN

For Adrienne, Alex and Jake

First published in Great Britain in 1995 by Hamlyn
an imprint of Reed Consumer Books Limited,
Michelin House
81 Fulham Road, London SW3 6RB
and Auckland, Melbourne, Singapore and Toronto

Reprinted 1996

EDITOR: **NINA SHARMAN**
ART EDITOR: **PRUE BUCKNALL**
PRODUCTION: **MICHELLE THOMAS**
EXECUTIVE EDITOR: **JUDITH MORE**
EXECUTIVE ART EDITOR: **LARRAINE SHAMWANA**
ART DIRECTOR: **JACQUI SMALL**

CRAFTS: **SOPHIE-JANE TILLEY**
TEXT: **SUSAN WELBY**
PHOTOGRAPHY: **MICHELLE GARRETT**
STEP-BY-STEP PHOTOGRAPHY: **POLLY WREFORD**

Text © Sophie-Jane Tilley and Susan Welby
© Reed International Books Limited 1995

A CIP record for this book is available from the British Library

ISBN 0 600 58636 7

The publishers have made every effort to ensure that all instructions given in this book
are accurate and safe, but they cannot accept liability for any resulting injury,
damage or loss to either person or property whether direct or consequential
and howsoever arising.

PRODUCED BY MANDARIN OFFSET
PRINTED AND BOUND IN CHINA

CONTENTS

CONTENTS

INTRODUCTION

The urge to model, bake and decorate dough is as traditional and as widespread as the practice of making bread itself. The ancient Egyptians, Romans and Greeks made dough figure offerings to their gods, and modelling dough decorations to commemorate religious festivals (particularly Christmas) is still a popular pastime in many European countries. Brightly coloured dough designs are sold on market stalls in South America, and tourist centres in Shanghai still demonstrate the traditional art of making enchanting dolls from twists of dyed dough. Salt-dough modelling is enjoying a revival in the USA and dough objects are beginning to make an appearance in British gift shops once again.

The availability of more sophisticated modelling materials, like ready-made and non-bake clays may have contributed to the decline in popularity of salt-dough. Convenience is bound to appeal to busy home-crafters, but the price of some modelling materials can be restricting. Salt-dough ingredients are very inexpensive to buy and quick to prepare, which means that you can afford to be adventurous in size and quantity and relaxed about the occasional mistake.

The projects in this book are meant to provide you with ideas, not hard-and-fast rules – so feel free to vary the designs and to add your own finishing touches. Suggestions about special paint effects, textures, cut-outs and alternative finishes are included in the introductions to many of the projects – use the photographs and instructions as guidelines, and your own ideas should soon develop along with your skill.

The standard items used for each craft can be found in most kitchens and any extra equipment mentioned is widely available. To give you more choice (and scope for invention), alternative or additional materials and tools are suggested wherever possible.

Hand-modelling is unpredictable by nature, so do think twice before throwing any "mistakes" away. If you are prepared to highlight, rather than hide slight variations and quirks, your work will be more original and unique to you. Aiming for perfection can be inhibiting, so relax and try not to see every flaw as a failure – production-line perfection isn't terribly inspiring and often lacks the charm and beauty of a hand-made craft.

Materials and Techniques

This section will give you a thorough grounding in all aspects of dough craft – from preparing the dough to applying highlights and decorative paint effects. Refer to this section whenever you have doubts or queries about modelling, relief work and baking – or simply browse through it to refresh your memory before embarking on the next project. Obviously, you want your craft work to look as good as possible, but don't be discouraged by unexpected results. Small flaws can add interesting dimensions to a project and an "accident" may produce an original texture or an unusual surface finish.

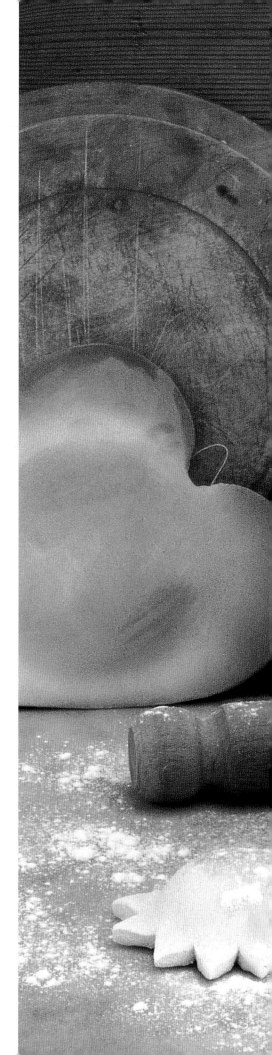

MAKING THE DOUGH

This book uses a traditional salt-dough mixture for all its projects. It is easier to stick to one recipe and, when made up and handled properly, this simple salt, flour and water mixture is very successful, extremely adaptable and behaves with a certain predictability, which is reassuring, especially when you are embarking on new projects.

Salt is an effective hardening agent. Although some experts add cooking oil or even wallpaper paste to their dough mixtures for extra smoothness and strength, the recipe below produces an excellent dough which handles and hardens successfully, without the addition of extra ingredients.

The basic recipe makes enough dough for one smallish project and two larger ones (a few small decorations with relief work and two bowls, for example). This may seem a lot, but baking more than one object at a time makes good economical and ecological sense. For less, or more dough, simply halve or double the ingredients given in the basic recipe accordingly. As a general rule, you should always use half the amount of salt to flour.

Ingredients

FLOUR – Plain white flour is used throughout this book. Use good-quality flour. Cheaper brands may be difficult to handle and can also vary widely in degrees of absorbency. You will be surprised how quickly you become accustomed to the look and feel of the dough you make, so once you have decided on a brand of flour, stay with it. Wholemeal flour produces interesting textured effects, but it tends to be heavier to handle and takes longer to bake than the plain white variety. Self-raising flour puffs up in the oven and should never be used for dough craft.

SALT – As long as it is finely ground, the cheapest salt available makes good dough. Buying in bulk is practical and economical and avoids frustrating last-minute shortages.

You will need
- Large mixing bowl
- Coffee mug
- Water jug
- Cool surface for kneading

THE BASIC RECIPE
- Two level mugs of plain white flour
- One level mug of finely ground salt
- About 355ml (12fl oz) lukewarm water

Method

Pour the flour and salt into a mixing bowl and combine thoroughly. Gradually add enough water to knead the mixture into a pliable ball. This may take more or less than the 355ml (12fl oz) of water in the recipe (depending on the flour you use and the temperature of the room). Judge the exact amount by feel – if the mixture becomes too sticky, add a little more flour. If it crumbles, add more water.

Kneading

The more you knead it, the smoother and more pliable salt dough becomes. Work the dough for at least ten minutes with slow, rhythmic movements, pushing it away from you with the heels of your hands, then folding it back on itself. Repeat the process again and again, turning the whole wad of

dough regularly. Well-prepared dough is firm, malleable and elastic enough to stretch into a soft, slightly bouncy "rope" when gently pulled.

TIPS
- The dough reacts best to a warm (but not hot) working environment. The dough itself is a good temperature gauge (it becomes soft, sticky and moist in an over-heated room).
- Keep your hands as cool and dry as possible when working with dough.
- Always work on a cool, dry surface.

Storing raw dough

Take as much dough as you need for the project in-hand, wrap the rest in cling-film (or seal it in an air-tight container) and store it in the refrigerator. When you are ready to use it, bring the stored dough back to room temperature by kneading it thoroughly.
- Dough gets soggy quite quickly and it doesn't store well for more than a day (or two days at the most), so only make as much as you can reasonably use.
- When putting dough to one side to use for a project underway, cover it with a dry cloth (only use a damp cloth when the dough needs moistening).

DOUGH PASTE

Dough paste plays an important part in salt-dough craft. It only takes seconds to prepare, so mix a fresh batch whenever you embark on a new project. A small, 3mm (1/8 in) paint brush is suitable for most pasting jobs. Although a nylon-bristled brush is perfectly adequate, the bristles should not be too stiff (in case they indent the dough) or too loose (in case the hairs fall out). Use a paint brush to apply the paste to raw dough in small amounts. If you paint on too much paste, your salt dough will become soggy and unmanageable, so use very little.

The thickness of the paste depends on the consistency needed for various techniques, but a watery mixture applied with a paint brush (to stick and seal dough pieces) is standard for all projects. Mix a thin paste and keep it to hand as you work – make up a thicker paste if and when you need it.

To attach relief work and decorations to a model, apply the paste sparingly to the underside of the shape to be attached. Then paint a little dough paste on the base area and join the two pieces together.

To fill gaps between layers of relief work, brush thicker dough paste into gaps until no joins are visible. If necessary, smooth over with a little plain water, applied with a paint brush, or use a small spatula to give a neat finish.

You can also use dough paste to correct mistakes. For example, if you need to cover unwanted indentations or surface scoring, brush a thicker paste over the affected area and smooth over the surface with a small spatula or a damp pastry brush.

To make dough paste
• When you have prepared your raw dough, tear off a peanut-sized piece of dough (for larger amounts of paste, tear off a bigger lump of dough).
• To make a standard, watery paste, put the dough into a saucer or lid and add lukewarm water, drop by drop. Mix until the dough becomes tacky and then add more water to thin it out.
• For a thicker paste, use the same method, but stop adding water when the paste is a soft, buttery consistency.

MATERIALS AND EQUIPMENT

Materials and equipment needed for individual projects are listed with their step-by-step instructions, but you may find a general list useful too. Most materials and equipment can be found around the house or at local hardware stores – either way, you won't have to travel far or visit specialist stockists to find them.

Standard list
• Salt dough
• Dough paste
• Cardboard for templates
• Non-stick baking sheet(s) (the raised edges on a standard baking tray can get in the way – a flat baking sheet is best)
• Ruler (for measuring dough thickness; when lightly floured, a ruler also makes a good cutter)
• Rolling pin
• Small kitchen knife
• Small wooden spatula, or flat, paddle-shaped modelling tool (for patting and smoothing edges and surfaces)
• Paint brush (not too large – for applying dough paste).

You will also need
(For certain projects)
• A long-bladed knife or pizza-cutting wheel (for cutting long strips of dough to equal widths and lengths)
• Lids of various sizes (round pastry cutters or small glasses can also be used)
• Oven-proof bowls to use as moulds
• Pastry cutters (to use as alternatives to templates)
• Pastry brush (to smooth and/or moisten larger surfaces)
• Tweezers (for handling small beads.)
• Cotton buds (for soaking-up excess moisture, cleaning mirrors)
• Wire, 1mm-thick (for hanging loops and threading)
• 30amp fuse wire
• Wire cutters
• Round-ended pliers (for bending wire)
• Small mirrors (mirror glass can be cut to size, or use old mirrors)
• Cork tiles, self-adhesive or plain felt (for backing)
• Adhesive
• Aluminium cooking foil (for moulded objects)
• Loose beads from broken brooches, necklaces and earrings, decorative buttons (for threaded decorations)
• Dried cloves (also for decoration)

MODELLING DECORATIONS

Surface decoration adds interest and texture to your work. Wherever possible, try to work on the baking sheet itself, this keeps the backs of your salt-dough pieces smooth (and transferring soft dough pieces from one surface to another can distort their shapes).

Do not add flour, water or grease to the baking sheet. If your dough has been prepared well, it should slide off the baking sheet easily when baked. If you must move any raw dough pieces, do so carefully, using a wide fish slice.

MODELLING SHELLS

These shells decorate the Shell Box on pages 50–1. Once you've picked up the general technique, you could try improvizing with a wider range of sea creatures. For example, star fish can be made with pastry cutters (or you could model them by hand).

To make cockleshells
1 Flatten a ball of dough into a fat disc.

2 Pinching one end between the thumb and forefinger of one hand, gently press the opposite end into a shell-shape.

3 Use a small knife to make shallow cuts on the surface of the shell and then score around the edges.

To make cochlea ("snail" or "screw-shells")
1 Roll a ball of dough into a short sausage.

2 Gently turn one end two or three times until it forms a spiral.

3 Use your finger to make a hole in the other end and turn upward to make a shell shape. Smaller shells can be made from small balls of dough, indented in the middle and pinched at both ends.

MODELLING AND ARRANGING LEAVES

Leaves and petals are used to decorate many of the dough-craft projects in this book. The trick is to make them look as natural as possible. If you are modelling by hand, don't try to produce exactly the same leaf or petal every time, but vary their shapes and sizes. If you are using templates to cut out leaves, their shapes will obviously be the same, but you can arrange them to look as realistic as possible.

Arranging and attaching leaves

Salt-dough leaves look best when they are arranged in a natural way (see Grapevine Basket, pages 26–9). Avoid laying leaves in flat, regimented lines – instead, add life to your arrangements by overlapping parts of some leaves and squeezing and twisting the tips of others. Leaves also look very attractive when draped over the edges of plaques and bowls. A small amount of dough paste is usually enough to attach raw dough decorations to a base shape, but you may find it useful to brush a little thickened dough paste on the underside of larger leaves (to reinforce any weak areas). Use thickened dough paste to fill gaps between shapes and to brush over any cracks.

To make vine leaves with a template

Roll the dough out to a thickness of about 5mm (¼in). Lay the vine leaf template (see page 130) on top of the dough and cut around it carefully. Smooth and tidy any rough edges. Add veins by gently pressing the knife blade into the dough. Score in the central, vertical line first, then add veins on either side of this line, work-

ing outward. When each scored line reaches the edge of the dough, press in to indent. With your thumb and forefinger, twist the ends of the leaves and tease them upward to vary their shapes.

To hand-model leaves

1 Flatten a small piece of dough. Either shape the leaf by hand, or cut and trim it into shape with a small knife. Smooth edges with the flat side of a knife blade or with a small spatula.

2 Add veins by gently pressing the blade of a small knife into the dough. Score in the central, vertical line first, then add veins on either side of this line. Where the scored lines reach the edge of the dough, press in to indent (this produces a fluted effect along the edges of the leaf).

OTHER DECORATIVE TECHNIQUES

Scoring the surface of salt dough is a technique used throughout this book. Not only is it a good way of adding texture and interest to a salt-dough model, it also provides attractive contrast lines when you come to paint it. Press the blade of a small kitchen knife gently across the surface of the dough.

Indenting the dough (with the end of a small paint brush or with a piece of wire) produces shallow holes which can be painted or used as sockets for decorative beads and small balls of salt dough. The point of a knife will produce smaller, sharper indentations. Indenting is also a useful way of creating features when modelling faces (see Gift for a New Baby, pages 126–7).

Flattening and patting edges and surfaces with a small wooden spatula (that has been slightly wetted) gives a smoother finish.

Cut-outs are simply shapes made with pastry cutters, lids from small jars or the rims of small glasses. Over-moist dough produces torn edges and soggy results, so make sure that the dough is flexible but not floppy before cutting your shape.

MAKING WIRE LOOPS

A piece of wire, embedded in a salt-dough base makes an effective hanging loop for displaying salt-dough wreaths, frames and decorations. Looping is also a good way of joining or reinforcing separate dough pieces securely. Loops of thinner, more flexible wire can be embedded in the backs of frames to anchor photographs in place (see Patchwork Frame, pages 56–7).

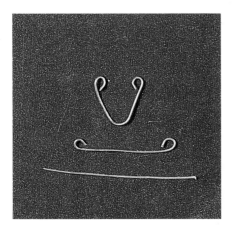

To make hanging loops

Cut a piece of 1mm-thick wire about 7cm (2³⁄₄in) long. Using round-ended pliers, curve the wire and curl each end into an open O-shape.

Push the loop into the dough base until both curled ends are hidden.

MOULDING

Draping dough over a raised surface adds a new dimension to modelling work. It brings flat shapes to life and responds beautifully to surface decoration. The secret of successful moulding lies in the preparation. Knead your dough thoroughly, to give it a pliable, almost elastic quality.

Moulded projects involve "half-baking". Simply bake the outside of the project until it has taken on the shape of the mould. When it is firm enough to handle (but still only half-baked), remove the mould and return the project to the oven to bake the inside. This process is described in more detail on the opposite page.

Moulding over foil shapes

Raw salt dough is extremely flexible, which means that it is perfectly suited to moulding over aluminium foil. This book uses various foil moulds to make containers and other decorative items. Moulds are made by scrunching sheets of foil into compact wads of various shapes (see the Moulded Moon above and on pages 46–7). The instructions for the relevant projects will give you an idea of the height and width of the shapes used, but as a general rule, use enough foil to squeeze into a densely packed mould (strong enough to support the dough during baking). If your mould is too large, squeeze harder to reduce its size, or tear off the excess foil. If it is too small, add more foil.

Moulding over oven-proof containers

Oven-proof bowls and dishes of various shapes and sizes make excellent salt-dough moulds. The instructions for the relevant projects will supply you with dimensions, but as long as the bowl or dish you choose is the right shape, you can vary the size of the project by using a larger, or smaller container. Oven-proof bowls with textured patterns, lipped edges or handles should be avoided.

The moulding technique itself is very straightforward. Just cover the outside of the oven-proof bowl with foil. Tuck the foil inside the bowl – the overlap should be about 5cm (2in) – and smooth the foil over the outside of the bowl until it is flat and as wrinkle-free as possible. Roll your dough out to the correct thickness, carefully drape it over the oven-proof container and trim around the edges (see the Ethnic Bowl above and on pages 64–7).

BAKING

Salt-dough baking is not an exact science. Ovens differ and cooking times may vary according to the thickness of a project, the number of projects baked at one time and the type of fuel used. When you have baked a few projects, you will have a better idea of exact baking times, according to the way your own oven performs.

Raw salt dough is rolled out to two standard thicknesses throughout this book. These are either 5mm (¼in) or 1cm (⅜in). The information on the right will give you an idea of the oven settings needed to bake projects with these standard base thicknesses. Bear in mind that relief work makes an object thicker, lengthening the baking process. Because of this, approximate baking times for certain types of project (heavily decorated, moulded and/or woven) are also listed.

If you are in any doubt, err on the side of caution. Baking slowly, on a low oven setting, protects against distortion. A slow, steady baking process will give you an idea of the way dough looks and feels as it hardens.

Pre-heat the oven and slide your baking sheet of uncooked dough onto the middle shelf. Use the oven temperatures and times printed right as a general guide, but don't worry too much about being exact. Your own judgement should soon tell you whether an object is "done", especially if you use the tap test.

The tap-test

As the dough cooks, it begins to harden and the surface starts to look drier and lighter in colour. When you think it's done, tap the object with your finger. If it sounds hollow, carefully slide a long-bladed knife or fish slice underneath to loosen it. Using an oven glove, turn the dough over carefully and tap its base. A hard texture and a hollow sound tell you that the object is ready (a spongy texture and a dull, thudding noise means that it needs more time in the oven).

APPROXIMATE BAKING TIMES AND TEMPERATURES

Thinner objects – 5mm (¼in) thick
150 °C (300°F), Gas Mark 2 for 3–4 hours
Aga 120°C (250°F) for 7 hours in warming oven

Thicker objects – 1cm (⅜in) thick.
150 °C (300°F), Gas Mark 2 for 6–7 hours
Aga 120°C (250°F) for 10 hours in warming oven

NOTE: Fan-assisted ovens tend to bake salt dough more quickly during the early stages. Take care to check your dough regularly. Projects decorated with solid pieces of dough relief, for example, the Traditional Fruit Basket (pages 36–7) and the Christmas Wreath (pages 91–3), will take about 10–12 hours to bake. Solid, hand-modelled items, for example, the African Doll (pages 70–5) and the Cherub Christmas decoration (pages 86–9) should be left in the oven for about 6–7 hours.

Cooling

Simply remove your baked project (on its baking sheet), from the oven and leave it to cool down. Avoid handling until cool (unless repair work is necessary – see page 18). In the case of projects with mirrors (for example, the Mermaid Mirror, pages 48–9) the oven should be turned off after baking and the project allowed to cool down gradually inside the oven. Avoid extreme changes in atmosphere. For example, if you have to move the dough to another room make sure that it is not exposed to steam, damp or cold. The dough must be allowed to cool completely before you paint or varnish it.

HALF-BAKING

All projects that use moulds need to be half-baked. Although this process can be fiddly, it is not complicated, but do take care when handling half-baked dough. Bake the project on the mould until it is firm enough to handle without distorting its shape or damaging its structure. Take it from the oven (close the oven door to retain heat), remove the mould and return the piece to the oven to finish baking through.

For projects baked on moulds without relief work, for example, the Ethnic Bowl (pages 64–7) and the Moulded Heart (pages 68–9), bake for about 4 hours at 150 °C (300°F) or Gas Mark 2 before removing the mould. Return to the oven for another 2½–3 hours to finish baking.

For projects with thick relief work, for example, the Shell Box (pages 50–1) add an extra ½ hour to the baking time before removing the foil mould, and about another hour to the final stage of baking.

For larger projects with thick relief work, for example, the Hen Lid (pages 82–3), add at least 1 hour to the baking time before removing the mould, and approximately 1 more hour to the final stage of baking.

Where half-baked components are attached to raw dough bases, for example, the Shell Box (pages 50–1) and the Horn of Plenty (pages 96–9), bake for about 4½ hours before removing the mould. After attaching the top to the base, return to the oven for about another 6 hours to finish baking.

Open-weave, moulded projects, for example, the Grape Vine Basket (pages 26–9) and the Hen Nest (pages 80–1), should be baked for about 6 hours before removing the mould and then returned to the oven for about 4–5 hours to finish baking.

BROWNING

This technique produces different degrees of colour, from pale gold to deep brown. Bake your project completely. Leaving the oven on, remove the cooked dough and make a mental note of its surface colour . Decide how much deeper you would like the colour to be. (Browning can happen quickly, so making decisions now will help you to react quickly and decisively when the dough reaches the right shade.)

Turn the oven up to the next setting. Return the project to the oven and watch closely as the increased heat deepens its colour. (If your oven has no

window, open the door regularly to check.) Remove the dough as soon as it has reached the desired shade. Avoid leaving your project too long – a very deep brown could turn black in seconds, burning your dough, or making it too brittle to use. Allow the dough to cool completely before painting and/or varnishing.

Browning will deepen a project's base-shade, providing a rich background for paint finishes. Use it as a colouring process on its own, or add a little spot-colour (see the the Moulded Heart above and on pages 68–9, the African Dolls, pages 70–5 or the Wheat Plaque, pages 94–5). Subtle shade changes produced by allowing the dough to blush naturally will give your work a dramatic finish, especially if you apply several coats of gloss varnish to deepen and enrich the dough's colour still further.

AIR DRYING

Although it takes longer (days and weeks, rather than hours), air drying saves on fuel bills and does not monopolise the oven. Again, exact drying times depend on the size and thickness

of the project and the surrounding temperature. Objects must be left undisturbed on a flat surface in a dry place – an airing cupboard is ideal. The temperature should be constant, but still keep a close eye on your dough as it may warp slightly.

On warm summer days, thinner objects can be dried outside and if you are lucky enough to live in a warm climate all year round, a shed or outhouse could be a perfect drying environment.

Dough should never be exposed to damp or extreme changes in temperature (see Preserving your Work).

FILLING AND REPAIRING

Small, hairline cracks in raw dough caused by bending and moulding, for example, can be repaired as and when they happen. Paint a little standard watery dough paste on the crack to seal it and continue modelling the dough.

Cracks sometimes appear as the dough starts to harden off and dry. This can happen before, or during baking. Heat is an excellent sealant, so repairing your dough while it is still warm (not hot) from the oven is often very successful. To fill hairline cracks, brush standard watery dough paste over the crack while the dough is still warm. The warmth from the dough should seal the crack quickly. Hairline cracks which appear after baking when the dough has cooled down should be sealed with a thicker paste.

To fill larger cracks, brush thicker dough paste into the crack (taking care not to press too hard) and then level-off any surface bumps by brushing a light coating of paste over the affected area. Brush on a little water to smooth out the paste. If necessary, return the object to the oven for a few minutes to seal. When the paste has hardened off (and the dough is cool), run your finger over the repair. If the surface is rough, rub over lightly with fine sandpaper before painting your model.

Where salt dough is built up in layers (cut-outs, petals or shells on a base, for example), any unsightly gaps and joins which appear after baking should be sealed and smoothed-over with thickened dough paste. Smooth over as before. After repairing, return the object to the oven. If you are still worried about the strength of a join, wait until the object is cool and use a little adhesive.

PAINTING

The paint finishes in this book are meant to supply you with ideas, not hard-and-fast rules. The easiest way to adapt any of the projects is to change the colours that appear in the photographs. If, for example, you prefer the idea of gold highlights on a black, rather than a red background, use the information on highlighting to guide you and apply your own choice of colour. If you can't commit yourself to a colour scheme straight away, make a rough drawing of the object and experiment on paper first.

To get an idea of the way certain colours (and thicknesses) of paint react to baked salt dough, roll out raw dough to a thickness of 1cm (³⁄₈in), cut into squares and bake. When these tiles of dough have cooled, use them to experiment with colour and paint effects. You could also varnish your painted tile

to see how colours intensify under a glossy surface. When you start painting the dough, be decisive. Water-based paints dry very quickly, so use bold brush strokes on large areas and paint evenly. Never overload your brush – the moisture could seep down into the salt dough.

Try restricting yourself to a certain number of colours (the choice is yours), but keep a couple in reserve to create contrast between textures.

Some objects lend themselves to groups of colours, but this need not be restricting. A simple leaf can be painted in shades of green, yellow, purple, brown, red-gold and burnt orange. Use darker shades of the same colour for definition – a deeper green on the veins of leaves, for example.

Tubes of watercolours and acrylics are easily mixed and diluted and are therefore excellent for varying colour-density. (Avoid oil-based products.)

PAINTING MATERIALS
Paints – a good range of watercolours, acrylics or other water-based paints
Brushes – buy the best you can – four or five, ranging from a thicker brush for stroking on large areas of background colour to a fine-bristled brush for detail (Cheaper brushes can be used, but only if their bristles are soft and firmly attached)
Cotton buds – for blotting excess moisture
Soft, lint-free rags or kitchen towel – for applying paint effects

PAINT TECHNIQUES
Colour washes
Applied in layers to build up colour gradually, colour washes create a gentle, finely blended effect. They can also be used as subtle background colours,

or as thin overlays (to tone-down stronger base colours). Washes are simply diluted paints, brushed over areas in sweeping strokes. Mix paint with water until it is fluid and loose enough to wash over the surface of the dough, leaving an even tint of colour.

Although washes are very watery, their colours should not be insipid. Judge the amount of water needed by adding enough to produce the desired shade.

Gold or silver washes are very effective when applied over other colours. Brushed over strong base coats, they produce a luxurious, even sheen and provide glimpses of the colour beneath (see the Moulded Stars below and on pages 42–3).

Dabbing on

The term dabbing on is used to describe the way patches of colour are applied as contrasts to base colours. Dabbing, rather than painting or brushing on colour produces a natural, soft-edged effect – this makes it ideal for "organic" decorations like leaves and fruits. Use a soft rag, a piece of kitchen paper or even your finger to dab a small amount of contrasting paint onto the dough. If necessary, dab off any excess paint with a clean piece

of rag or kitchen towel. The fruits on the Christmas Wreath (above and on pages 91–3) and in the Traditional Fruit basket (pages 36–7) are painted and then dabbed with darker, and lighter colours for contrast.

Brushing on highlights

Highlights draw attention to areas of texture or colour. The cornflowers on the Wheat Sheaf Plaque (pages 94–5) have been highlighted in blue. A highlight can be any shade, as long as it compliments the base colour. Gold and silver add a subtle sheen to decorations – but the trick is to know when to stop. Too many highlights can swamp a design, so be selective about the areas

you treat. Apply a tiny amount of gold paint with an almost-dry paint brush. Stroke your brush over the chosen area and wipe over quickly with a piece of kitchen towel to leave slivers of highlights. (Highlights can also be dabbed on with a soft rag, or with your finger.)

Toning-down and blending

Water-based paint dries quickly, which can prove a problem if you are unsure about the finish you have produced. As long as you know how to tone colours down and blend edges, minor mistakes need not be a problem.

If a colour wash looks too pale and insipid, simply apply more washes, until you are happy with the result.

A dark colour can often be muted by washing over with a lighter, complementary shade. Or, tone down a colour by brushing on a little water and dabbing immediately with clean rag while the paint is still damp (this should lift off some of the paint).

If painting produces a hard-edged finish, apply a complimentary colour wash (or apply plain water). Gently dab at any hard-definition lines with a cotton bud or small piece of rag to blend and soften the effect.

Burnishing

A "polishing" technique, burnishing produces a muted, antique effect. This finish gives glittering colours like gold a more subtle sheen (see Moulded Sun, pages 46–7). You must work quickly, as the base coat should still be damp when you apply the burnish. With a soft rag, a piece of kitchen towel or your finger, dab tiny amounts of black paint (diluted with water) over a (still-damp) gold-painted area. Before the black paint is completely dry, rub with a soft rag (using small, circular polishing movements).

This technique was used on the Gift for a New Baby shown above and on pages 126–7.

VARNISHING

Not only does it help to seal and protect your work, varnish also adds a veneer of depth and richness to surface colours and brings out the natural tones of baked, unpainted salt dough. Careless varnishing can ruin a beautifully-painted object, so apply each coat carefully, using a smaller brush for fine-relief and decorative areas.

Whether you use gloss or matte varnish is up to you. Some people prefer a high-definition shine on everything, while others go for a more subtle effect. The projects in this book are finished with gloss polyurethane varnish, but a matte finish can be just as effective.

- Cover a flat surface with newspaper (to protect it).
- Apply each coat carefully, using even strokes and enough varnish to cover the surface evenly. If the varnish drips off the brush, you are using too much.
- Each object will need five or six coats of varnish.
- Varnish the backs of projects to seal and protect them.
- Leave each coat to dry completely, before applying the next.
- When varnishing more than one object at a time, make a simple chart to record the number of coats applied to each.
- Always clean brushes thoroughly after use.

Egg white is a natural-looking varnish for traditional, unpainted salt-dough objects (like wreaths). Brush the egg white on before baking. This finish is not as long-lasting as chemical varnish.

Varnishing tools
- Decorator's brush, 1cm (½in), for larger objects
- Paint brush – for smaller objects (a nylon-bristle brush is suitable, but do check that the bristles are firmly attached)
- Chopstick or wooden spoon-handle – to stir varnish
- Polyurethane varnish (clear, gloss or matte)
- Turpentine – for cleaning brushes

FINISHING YOUR WORK
Painting and varnishing the backs of finished pieces will protect your models, but if you're worried about filled cracks, general repairs or an uneven finish, you may prefer to cover the backs of plaques, frames, mirrors and some decorations. Use (thin) cork tiles as backing. Cut cork to size and glue into place. Felt makes a good backing, again, cut to size and stick. Or, try a short-cut and use sticky-backed felt that can be peeled and stuck into place.

PRESERVING YOUR WORK
Although it is surprisingly strong and long-lasting, salt dough is also extremely susceptible to changes in temperature and to damp. Varnishing your work carefully will help to seal and protect it, but you should avoid damp atmospheres like bathrooms and steamy kitchens (or areas in kitchens which become steamy – around cookers and work surfaces where a kettle is in use). Never display salt dough in rooms where the temperature fluctuates from one extreme to another (for example, sun-rooms, storm porches or unheated conservatories). Avoid placing salt dough too near radiators or heaters. Window ledges may seem ideal places to display your work, but they can become very cold and damp.

SAFETY
There is a very real danger of children mistaking salt dough for cakes or biscuits and this can be especially hazardous where crafts contain wires. Make sure that finished decorations and hanging plaques are kept well out of reach. Keep lids on varnish and sharper tools out of reach. Take normal safety precautions when baking.

Nature's Gifts

The fresh colours of spring, the brilliance of summer, the rich hues of autumn or the cool shades of winter, whatever the season, nature provides the inspiration for these designs.

The simplest images are often the most effective. Sometimes, just the shape of a leaf or the colour of a plant will spark off an idea.

Although the salt dough projects in this section are easy to reproduce exactly, they are also designed to provide you with ideas and inspiration. Vary the sizes and shapes of the individual pieces, or add some personal touches to give your work a truly original finish.

LEAF DISHES

These dishes are designed to be practical and decorative. Fill them with sweets or chocolates for special occasions, or use them as pot-pourri holders. Once you have mastered the art of working on a mould, you can re-create your favourite leaf shapes by adapting our instructions. Either cut your leaf freehand, or vary the size of the template provided to make a larger or smaller dish. Nothing could be more simple, and dramatic than the shape and colours of a leaf, especially if you choose deep, rich autumnal shades. Brush washes of diluted paint over your dish to build-up a natural-looking surface finish, then highlight the leaf's shape and texture by dabbing on deeper colours. For more information on painting see Materials and Techniques, pages 19–20.

MATERIALS AND EQUIPMENT

Salt dough (see page 12)
Dough paste (see page 13)
Non-stick baking sheet
Rolling pin
Leaf dish template (page 130)
Small kitchen knife
Small wooden spatula
*Oven-proof dish (about 16cm (6½in)
in diameter)*
Aluminium foil
Pastry brush
*Brushes for applying dough paste, paints
and varnish*
Rag or paper towel to apply paint finishes
Water-based paints
Gloss polyurethane varnish

1 Cover the outside of an oven-proof bowl with foil, folding about 5cm (2in) of the foil over the lip of the bowl. Flatten the foil until it is smooth all over. Roll out the dough to a thickness of about 5mm (¼in). Lay the template on the dough and cut around it to make the leaf shape.

2 Lift the dough leaf carefully and lay it over the upside-down, foil-covered bowl. Smooth with a damp (not wet) pastry brush, taking care not to stretch the dough out of shape as you do so. Pat and smooth any rough edges with a spatula or damp pastry brush. Using a small kitchen knife, score the veins onto the leaf. Indent the edges of the leaf for a scalloped effect.

3 Bake until the surface is dry looking and hard enough to handle without distorting (see pages 17–18). Remove the oven-proof bowl and carefully peel the foil away. Place your dough leaf dish right-way-up on the baking sheet and return it to the oven to finish baking.

4 Paint the dish with a wash of brown paint. Don't worry about surface cracks – the paint will sink into them, adding to the "veined" effect. Now dilute some orange paint with a little water. Dip a soft rag into the paint and dab it over the leaf. When the paint is dry, varnish your dish.

GRAPE VINE BASKET

Although it looks elaborate, this basket is surprisingly easy to make. As long as you weave a good, strong lattice surface and flatten it out evenly, attaching the vine leaves and grapes could not be simpler. Don't let size restrict you, the basket pictured here was moulded on a 18cm (7in) oven-proof bowl, but smaller, or larger bowls are just as effective. Although it is easier to cut out and score more than one leaf at a time, take care to cover any shapes that are not in immediate use with a cloth, to prevent them drying out. The decorative leaves and grapes on the basket should look lush and natural. Drape grapes in

succulent bunches. Lift, twist and overlap the edges of the vine leaves, arranging some at angles and curving others over the lip of the basket. Then paint your bowl in rich shades and brush or dab-on contrasting colours for a sumptuous finish. Alternatively, you could brown off your bowl and just paint the leaves and fruit, as in the bowl on pages 22–3. When the paint is dry, apply thin coats of gloss varnish. Allow each coat to dry thoroughly before applying the next and the result will be a deep, long-lasting sheen. For more information on baking, painting and varnishing see Materials and Techniques, pages 17–21.

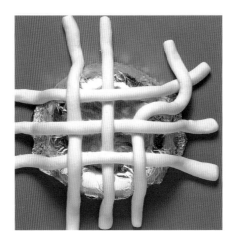

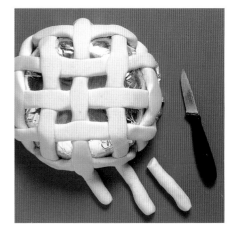

1 Cover the outside of an oven-proof bowl with foil – about 5cm (2in) of foil should overlap inside the bowl. Smooth the foil all over. Roll sausage-shaped dough strips by hand; the strips should be a little longer than your (upside-down) foil-covered bowl. Although you will eventually flatten the dough strips with a rolling pin, try to roll each strip to an even thickness of about 1cm (³⁄₈in). Roll a few strips at a time and cover the rest of your dough to prevent it drying out.

2 Start weaving your bowl by positioning a cross of two strips in the centre of the (upside-down) oven-proof bowl. Now add more strips, weaving them over and under as you go. Make the gaps between your lattice-work as even as possible. These strips will spread when they are flattened, so leave enough space between them as you weave.

3 Once the bowl is covered in woven strips, lightly roll over the whole area with a rolling pin (this will give you an even surface for decoration). The strips should now be flattened to a thickness of about 5mm (¼in) each. Trim any excess dough away from the rim. Gently squeeze the edges of the overlapping pieces so that they stick neatly together.

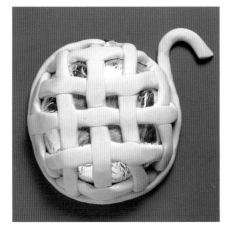

4 Roll an edging strip by hand, to run around the circumference of the bowl. Press it lightly into place, or attach it with a little dough paste. This edging strip will cover any untidy ends.

5 To make the grapes, roll oval balls of dough (about 1cm (³⁄₈in) long). Arrange the balls in bunches. Position a bunch of grapes on every other vertical lattice strip (below the edging strip). Attach with dough paste. Next, gently flatten the edging strip by hand.

6 To make vine leaves, roll dough to a thickness of about 5mm (¼in). Cut around leaf template. With your knife score veins on the leaf. Repeat. Arrange leaves around the edge of the bowl, overlapping some and twisting the tips of others. Attach with dough paste. Arrange more leaves around the outside of the bowl. Attach with dough paste. Bake the upside-down bowl.

7 When the bowl is hard enough to handle without distorting, take it from the oven, remove the oven-proof bowl and peel away the foil. Return to the oven right way up and finish baking. When cool, apply a wash of dark green paint to the inside of the bowl and when this is dry, turn the bowl over and paint the lattice part of the bowl in the same colour.

8 Paint the leaves with a wash of light green paint. While the wash is still damp, dab on a little brown or dark green paint with a brush or soft rag. Paint a purple wash over the grapes. Before the wash is dry, dab on a little brown or darker paint for contrast. When dry, varnish.

MATERIALS AND EQUIPMENT
Salt dough (see page 12)
Dough paste (see page 13)
Non-stick baking sheet
Rolling pin
Vine leaf template (page 130)
Small kitchen knife
Small wooden spatula
Oven-proof bowl
Aluminium foil
Pastry brush
Brushes for applying dough paste, paints and varnish
Rag or paper towel to apply paint finishes
Water-based paints
Gloss polyurethane varnish

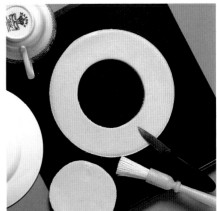

1 Working straight onto the baking sheet, roll out dough to a thickness of about 5mm (¼in). Lay your plate on top of the dough and cut around it. Now stamp a hole in the centre by pressing down on a lid or a glass. Try to make the dough area of the ring about 5cm (2in) across. Tidy any rough edges. Smooth the surface with a damp pastry brush.

2 To make sunflower centres, roll a ball of dough, flatten it with your thumb and position this on your wreath. Do this four times. (Arrange the centres at equal intervals around the wreath.) Attach with dough paste.

SUNFLOWER WREATH

This sunflower wreath uses strong colours and varied textures to make a bright impression. Follow the instructions to create your wreath base and sunflowers then, using the template, make and attach the leaves. Use dried cloves to give the sunflower centres a natural finish – other dried spices, small beads or balls of painted salt dough are good alternatives. You may prefer the subtle tones of baked dough to the bright colours used here. If this is the case, keep a close eye on the baking process. Wait until the heat flushes the leaves and petals a deeper shade of gold then let the wreath cool down completely before sealing it with varnish for a deep, lasting sheen.

MATERIALS AND EQUIPMENT
Salt dough (see page 12)
Dough paste (see page 13)
Non-stick baking sheet
Rolling pin
Small leaf template (page 131)
Small kitchen knife
Small wooden spatula
Pastry brush
Plate to cut around for wreath shape (about 20cm (8in) in diameter)
Lid or glass to stamp out central hole (about 10cm (4in) in diameter)
Cloves for decoration
Brushes for applying dough paste, paints and varnish
Rag or paper towel to apply paint finishes
Water-based paints
Gloss polyurethane varnish

3 To make petals, roll small balls of dough between your palms, flatten and shape them into ovals (about 1cm (³⁄₈in) long and 5mm (¼in) thick). Arrange petals around each sunflower centre. Attach with dough paste. Score lines on petals with a sharp knife.

4 Push dried cloves (flower end up) into the sunflower centres. To make the leaves, roll out dough to a thickness of about 5mm (¼in) and cut around the template. Using the photograph as a guide, arrange the leaves. Twist and overlap some of the leaves to make them look natural. Attach with dough paste. Score veins on leaves with a sharp knife.

5 Bake your wreath (see pages 17–18 for information on baking). When cool, paint the base shape of the wreath with diluted brown paint. Cover the leaves with a wash of green paint and with a soft rag dab on a little black paint for a natural effect. Paint the sunflower petals a vibrant yellow and leave the centres their natural dough colour. When the paint is dry, varnish the sunflower wreath.

BEE AND FLOWER MOBILE

Although it is not designed to spin and flutter in the breeze, this bee and flower mobile should sway gently when touched. Hang it near a window or a lamp, and the light will make the colours even more vibrant. The photographs are here to guide you, and you can introduce your own ideas and finishing touches to produce a very original finish. Add more beads and bells, or use sugarcraft cutters to make tiny dough shapes for threading. Each flower, leaf and bee is simple to model. To copy the mobile exactly, you should make two large flowers, two medium flowers and two small ones. (All the flowers are modelled in exactly the same way.)

As long as you calculate the right amount of wire for the finished mobile, you can thread on as many decorations as you like.

MATERIALS AND EQUIPMENT

Salt dough (see page 12)
Dough paste (see page 13)
Non-stick baking sheet
Rolling pin
Ruler
Small kitchen knife
Small wooden spatula
Pastry brush
1mm-thick wire, about 2m (2yd 6in)
Wire cutters
Round-ended pliers
Beads, bell for decoration
Brushes for applying dough paste, paints and varnish
Rag or paper towel to apply paint finishes
Water-based paints
Gloss polyurethane varnish

1 Working straight onto the baking sheet (so that the flowers' backs are flattened), roll a ball of dough between your palms. Flatten the top gently with your thumb or palm. Indent the centre by pressing down with your thumb or forefinger. Using the blunt edge of a knife, score indentations to make petal sections, and a small circle to form the centre of the flower. If necessary, go over each indentation a second time to make good, strong dividing lines. Complete the flower by rolling a small ball of dough and attaching it to the flower shape with dough paste. Make two large flowers about 4cm (1½in) across, two medium flowers about 3cm (1¼in) across and two small ones about 2.5cm (1in) across. Each flower is about 1cm (⅜in) thick when flattened out.

2 Make four leaves about 4cm (1½in) long and about 2cm (¾in) across. Roll out dough to a thickness of about 1cm (⅜in) and cut out leaf shapes with a knife. Tidy any rough edges with a spatula. Score in veins. Now make two larger leaves about 6cm (2½in) long and 1cm (⅜in) thick). Press them together (a little dough paste may help). Attach one of the large flowers to the middle of this leaf shape.

3 Working straight onto the baking sheet (so that the bees have flat backs), roll balls of dough about 2 x 2cm (¾ x ¾in) and about 1cm (⅜in) thick. Roll smaller balls of dough, shape them into wings and attach two to each ball-shaped bee. Make six bees.

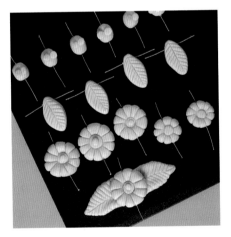

4 Guide a piece of 8cm (3¼in) wire through the middle of each flower and bee shape. Thread wires through the top of each leaf-shape. Leave enough wire jutting out at either end of each shape to turn during baking. Bake, turning the wires occasionally (see pages 17–18).

5 When cool, paint each piece according to the photograph, or use your own paint-effects. (Hold each dough piece by its wire to make painting easier.) When the paint is dry, varnish the dough pieces. When the varnish is dry, remove the wires carefully.

6 To calculate the length of wire for vertical threading, lay all the shapes in the correct order on a flat surface. Leave space in between for beads. Measure the total length of shapes and beads (about 32cm (13in) if you're following the measurements exactly). Add an extra 6cm (2½in) for a hanging loop at the top and an extra 3cm (1¼in) at the bottom for the bell and locking-loop. Cut your length of wire with the wire cutters.

7 To thread the mobile vertically, first thread the bell and bend a locking loop below it with your pliers. Then thread beads and dough shapes onto the wire.

8 Calculate the length of wire for the horizontal part of the mobile in the same way as you did for the vertical threading. Cut the correct length of wire. Before threading your shapes, twist the centre of the (unthreaded) wire around the wire remaining at the top of the vertical (threaded) piece. Turn the wire a couple of times, making sure that some still remains jutting up from the vertical. Now thread shapes along the right and left of the horizontal wire. When you've finished threading, bend locking loops at each end of the horizontal part of your mobile. Twist the remaining wire at the top of the mobile into a hanging loop.

TRADITIONAL FRUIT BASKET

Piled high with delicious-looking fruit, this traditional basket brims with nature's harvest. Size need not restrict you – if you would like to make a larger or smaller basket, enlarge or reduce the size of the template accordingly. Once you have cut out the base-shape and added the decorative wicker-work, you can alter the arrangement and contents of the basket to suit your own taste or even the season of the year. The overall impression should be full-blown and luxurious, so brush on touches of contrasting colour to give the fruit a ripening blush. Curl leaves over the lip of the basket and arrange grapes and nuts in groups between larger fruits for a sumptuous effect.

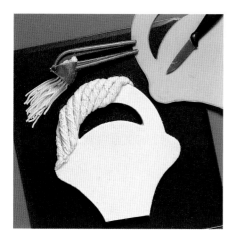

1 Roll out dough to a thickness of about 1cm (³⁄₈in). Cut around the template. Smooth and tidy any rough edges. Squeeze balls of dough through a garlic press. Twist each bunch of squeezed strands twice and arrange on the handle.

2 Now make a rim for the basket, using the same method. But this time, lay your twisted strands end to end. A little dough paste may help you to attach the strands. The rim defines the area above which you will lay the fruit.

3 With the blade of a knife, score a woven effect onto the basket. Work down the basket scoring straight, horizontal lines. Then score diagonal lines across the basket, from left to right and another series of lines from right to left.

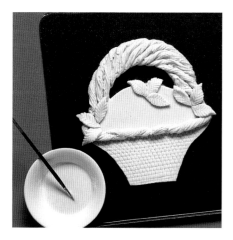

4 Roll out more dough, this time to a thickness of 5mm (¼in). Cut around the leaf template to make nine leaves. Tidy any rough edges. Score in veins. Arrange two groups of three leaves and attach one group to the right and the other to the left-hand corner of the basket. Twist the tips of the leaves to make them look natural. Now attach another group of three leaves at the top centre of the basket (see photograph).

5 The oranges and apples are simply balls of dough, about 3cm (1¼in) across. Arrange and attach them to the basket shape. Press dried cloves into the fruit – flower side up for the oranges and stalk side up for the apples. You will eventually paint these balls of dough their appropriate colours.

6 The grapes are smaller balls of dough, arranged in bunches. Tease the ends of dough balls into points to make plums. The nuts are smaller, circular balls of dough. Arrange and attach the plums, grapes and nuts. Cut single leaves out of dough and use them to fill any gaps in your fruit arrangement. Attach them with dough paste and score in veins. Bake (see pages 17–18 for information on baking). Paint and when dry, varnish.

1 Working straight onto the baking sheet, roll out the dough to a thickness of about 1cm (³/₈in). Place your templates on top of the dough and cut carefully around each shape. Smooth and tidy any rough edges with a spatula or damp pastry brush.

MATERIALS AND EQUIPMENT

Salt dough (see page 12)
Dough paste (see page 13)
Non-stick baking sheet
Bird and heart template (page 131)
Rolling pin
Ruler
Small kitchen knife
Small wooden spatula
Pastry brush
1mm-thick wire, about 34cm (13¹/₂in)
Wire cutters
Round-ended pliers
Beads, bell for decoration
Brushes for applying dough paste, paints and varnish
Water-based paints
Gloss polyurethane varnish

BIRD HANGING

Simple shapes are often the most rewarding to decorate. You can transform dough cut-outs just by painting them in spectacular colours and adding delicate patterns. This bird hanging is also a good way of displaying beads or fancy buttons. Or why not make your own beads? Simply roll small balls of dough, pierce them with wire and turn the wires (to keep the holes open) during baking. Paint the beads in bright, jewel-like colours and then thread them carefully onto the wire with the bird. The result is an original hanging, decorated with individual style.

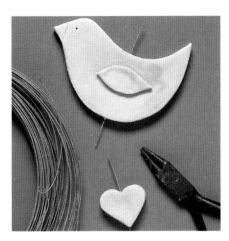

2 Attach wing to body of bird, sealing around edges with a small amount of dough paste. With your knife, gently score a dividing line between the bird's beak and head. Indent the eye shape with the end of your paint brush.

3 Taking care not to distort the dough, carefully guide a 9cm (3½in) length of wire down through the bird's body. Then guide a 6cm (2½in) length of wire through the dough heart. Bake (see pages 17–18), turning the wires about every 15 minutes to keep the threading holes open.

4 When baked, allow the dough to cool and then use your round-ended pliers to withdraw the wires. Paint the bird and heart using the photographs as a guide. When dry, varnish.

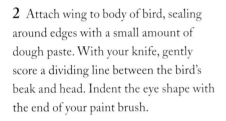

5 To calculate the length of wire for final threading, lay the bird, beads, heart and bell on a flat surface. Allow enough wire for bending into a hanging loop at the top and a smaller, locking loop at the bottom, then cut the wire to the correct length. Bend a tight, locking loop at the bottom and thread the bell, heart, beads and bird onto the wire. Shape the top of the wire into a hanging loop.

Essential Elements

The sea and the sky are limitless sources of inspiration. Whether you are making something as ethereal as a star, or simply trying to model a seashell by hand – remember that the unexpected can produce interesting results, so don't strive too hard for perfection.

The designs that follow use moulding, hand modelling and decorative relief-work to produce very original finishes. The instructions show you how to lift flat shapes into new dimensions, simply by mastering a few, basic skills. Spectacular paint effects are just as easy, so let the elements inspire you to produce touches of pure fantasy.

MOULDED STARS

One golden star is enough to brighten the corner of any room, or why not make a whole galaxy to decorate a wall? These stars are created by using foil moulds (page 16 has more tips on moulding). The rules are simple – just knead your dough thoroughly before rolling it out; keep the raw dough shape central when you drape it over the foil dome, and don't strive too hard for perfection. A few surface bumps will make the finished effect even more interesting. Templates are provided, but you could easily adapt them to suit your own designs. Or roll the dough out, drape it over the mould and then cut out your own edging pattern.

MATERIALS AND EQUIPMENT

Salt dough (see page 12)
Dough paste (see page 13)
Non-stick baking sheet
Rolling pin
Star template (page 132)
Small kitchen knife
Small wooden spatula
Aluminium foil
Pastry brush
Brushes for applying dough paste, paints and varnish
Rag or paper towel to apply paint finishes
Water-based paints
Gloss polyurethane varnish

1 Working straight onto the baking sheet, roll the dough out to a thickness of about 5mm (¼in). Lay the template on top of the dough and cut around the star shape carefully.

2 Roll some foil between your palms to make a ball. Flatten one side of the foil to make a dome shape. The dome should measure about 6cm (2½in) across the base and be about 2.5cm (1in) high.

Use the template provided or vary the star design by draping the dough over the foil mould and cutting out the rays free-hand, as pictured above.

3 Place the foil dome on the baking sheet. Lay the dough on top of the dome, taking care to make it central. Gently pat and flatten the star's rays on the baking sheet. Use the end of your paint brush to pierce a hanging hole in one of the rays. Smooth any rough edges with a damp pastry brush or spatula. Half-bake, remove the foil mould and return to the oven to finish baking (see pages 17–18).

4 Allow to cool. Either use gold paint, or apply an orange paint as a base, followed by a wash of gold (see pages 19–20 for information on painting). When the paint is dry, varnish.

MOULDED SUN

A burnished-gold paint finish gives this sun a luxurious sheen. Its contours gleam in daylight and glow mysteriously under artificial light. Although it is moulded on foil in exactly the same way as the stars on pages 42–3, the sun is larger so the dough is thicker and the rays are longer. Blend the features into the base shape carefully, but bear in mind that hand modelling is not an exact process. If you want to vary the sun's shape and facial expression, go ahead. Make the rays surrounding the face as eye-catching as possible. Surface ripples and waves look very effective, especially when they are painted and varnished, so do be as adventurous as you can.

MATERIALS AND EQUIPMENT
Salt dough (see page 12)
Dough paste (see page 13)
Non-stick baking sheet
Rolling pin
Sun template (pages 132–3)
Small kitchen knife
Small wooden spatula
Aluminium foil
Pastry brush
Brushes for applying dough paste, paints and varnish
Rag or paper towel to apply paint finishes
Water-based paints
Gloss polyurethane varnish

1 Working straight onto the baking sheet, roll dough out to about 1cm (³⁄₈in). Lay the template on top of the dough and cut around the shape.

2 When the dough is on its foil mould, vary the shape of the sun's rays by squeezing and shaping them between your thumb and forefinger until they become uneven and wavy. Taking care not to distort the dough, score lines down the rays.

3 Roll out four small sausage shapes for the eyebrows and eyelids, two sausage shapes for the lips and a slightly thicker sausage for the nose. Roll two small balls for the nostrils and two small (flattened) balls for the eyes. Position the features and attach them with a little dough paste. Shape and blend the nostrils into the end of the nose and press holes into the underside with the end of a paint brush.

4 Mould the chin by blending the edges of a dough ball into the dough base. Press contours into the face with your thumbs. Use the end of your paint brush to pierce a hanging hole in one of the rays. Half-bake, remove the foil mould and return to the oven to finish baking. (For more information on baking see pages 17–18). When you have painted your sun, varnish.

To paint, apply a thin wash of gold paint. While the paint is still damp, dab on a little black paint. Rub off in small, circular movements for a mottled effect.

MOULDED MOON

Shimmering colour washes will add a supernatural touch to this salt dough moon, especially if the surface is rippled and uneven.

Once you have draped the raw dough over your foil mould, gently squeeze the moon into a crescent-shape by hand. Your fingers will pucker the dough as you squeeze, automatically producing the right effect. Then use your thumbs to indent the surface. Blend the moon's features into the dough shape carefully and take care when baking. (Heavily-contoured shapes can easily overcook.) Try to keep the underside level at all times, but don't worry if the finished moon doesn't hang absolutely flat against the wall. Any shadows that it casts will simply add to the three-dimensional effect.

1 Make a crescent-shaped foil mould measuring approximately 22cm (8½in) in length and 8cm (3¼in) at the widest point. (See pages 16 for tips on moulding on foil.)

2 Roll dough out to about 1cm (⅜in) and carefully lay it over the foil mould. Cut around the mould and smooth any rough edges with a spatula or damp pastry brush. Add interest and surface contours to the basic moon shape by gently squeezing to distort it. Pucker the surface by pressing-in contours with your thumbs. Make an indentation for the mouth.

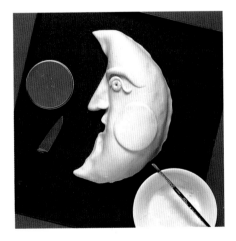

3 To model the moon's face, roll a cone-shaped piece of dough for the nose and flatten the underside. Attach the nose to the moon with a little dough paste and blend the edges into the overall shape. Roll two dough sausages for the eyebrow and eyelid. Curl and attach them to the moon, using a little dough paste.

4 Roll a ball for the eye, flatten it and attach with dough paste. Indent the eye with the end of a paint brush. Roll out a piece of dough about 2.5mm (⅛in) thick. Use a glass or a jar lid to press out a circle for the cheek. Attach with dough paste. Half-bake, remove the foil and return to the oven to finish baking (see pages 17–18).

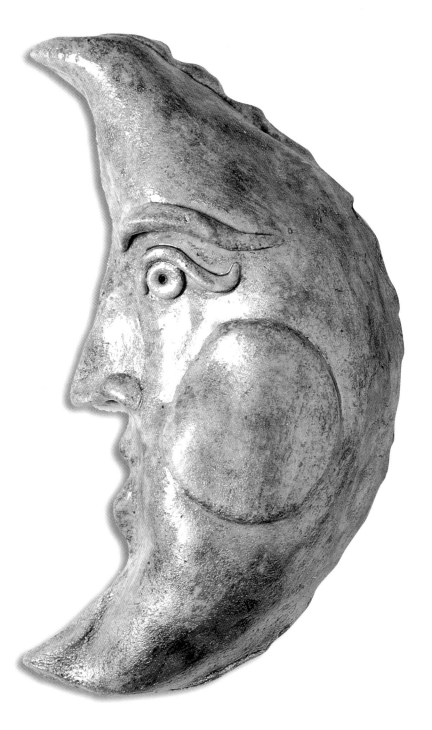

MATERIALS AND EQUIPMENT

Salt dough (see page 12)

Dough paste (see page 13)

Non-stick baking sheet

Rolling pin

Ruler

Small kitchen knife

Small wooden spatula

Aluminium foil

Pastry brush

Glass or lid to stamp out cheek

Brushes for applying dough paste, paints
and varnish

Rag or paper towel to apply paint finishes

Water-based paints

Gloss polyurethane varnish

*To paint the moon, apply a thin wash of
blue paint. While the blue paint is still
damp, cover with a wash of silver
paint. Using a soft rag or paper towel,
blend both colours together while still
damp. Dab on tiny amounts of black
paint. Rub off in small, circular movements. When the paint is completely dry,
varnish. (For information on painting
see pages 19–20.)*

MERMAID MIRROR

This mirror makes a perfect gift for those fascinated by the mystery of the sea. As long as you pre-heat your oven to a low setting and leave the dough to cool down in the oven after baking, this project can be baked with the mirror embedded into it. And because the edges of the mirror will be hidden by a rolled-dough frame, you could use a piece of broken mirror instead of a brand new one. To convey the impression of shimmering sea water, brush washes of green paint onto the base of the plaque and then rub-over with gold. Emphasize the relief-work on the mirror by colouring the mermaids in contrasting shades and burnish with highlights of gold. For more information on painting see Materials and Techniques, pages 19–20.

MATERIALS AND EQUIPMENT

Salt dough (see page 12)

Dough paste (see page 13)

Non-stick baking sheet

Rolling pin

Ruler

Mermaid template (page 133)

Small kitchen knife

Small wooden spatula

Pocket-sized mirror (about 6cm (2½in) wide and 3mm (⅛ in) thick)

Garlic press

Pastry brush

Brushes for applying dough paste, paints and varnish

Water-based paints

Gloss polyurethane varnish

1 Roll out dough to a thickness of about 5mm (¼in). Using a ruler, cut out a rectangle measuring about 14 x 19cm (5½ x 7½in). Smooth and tidy any rough edges with a spatula or a damp pastry brush. Now score a border about 5mm (¼in) in from the edge of your dough rectangle.

2 Position the mirror in the middle of the top half of the rectangle. (The lower edge of the mirror should be about 10cm (4in) up from the scored line at the foot of the rectangle.) Press the mirror into the dough gently (don't press too hard, or you will distort the dough).

3 Roll a sausage of dough (about 1cm (⅜in) thick) by hand. Attach the sausage around the mirror with dough paste. Make sure that it is firmly attached and that its edges are sealed. Score the inner edge and make indentations all the way around the frame with the end of a paint brush.

4 Roll out dough to a thickness of about 5mm (¼in). Cut around the mermaid template. Tidy any rough edges with a spatula or damp pastry brush and put this dough shape aside. Now turn the template over and cut around it to make another mermaid in reverse. Tidy any rough edges. Using the photograph as a guide, arrange the mermaids on the base shape and attach them with dough paste.

5 To make the mermaids' hair, push balls of dough through a garlic press. Arrange and attach these strands, using the photograph as a guide. To make the arms, roll two sausages of dough (about 6cm (2¼in) long and 1cm (⅜in) wide) and position one on each mermaid. Using a damp paint brush, press and blend the edges into the bodies of the mermaids.

6 Score a line across each body to define the start of the tail. To give the impression of scales, make indentations all over each mermaid's tail using the end of a paint brush. Bake in a pre-heated oven at the coolest setting (see pages 17–18 for information on baking). When the dough is baked, switch off and leave it inside the oven to cool down. Paint and varnish.

SHELL BOX

This container is perfect for storing loose beads, small buttons, a collection of shells or anything that is too precious to leave lying around.

When you have constructed the basic box shape, refer to page 14 for instructions on hand-modelling the decorative shells. Then arrange the shells in natural-looking groups for a finish that is realistic enough to have been swept ashore by the sea.

A wash of orange paint will produce a warm, pearly effect. Dab tiny amounts of black paint onto small areas, then rub off immediately, leaving subtle highlights.

Unpainted dough can be extremely effective too. Carefully brown the dough off in the oven. When the shells have flushed a deeper shade, remove the box and let it cool down. Finally, use a gloss varnish to give the shell box a rich, lustrous sheen.

For more information on baking and painting see Materials and Techniques, pages 17–20.

MATERIALS AND EQUIPMENT

Salt dough (see page 12)
Dough paste (see page 13)
Non-stick baking sheet
Rolling pin
Ruler
Stiff cardboard
Adhesive tape
Small kitchen knife
Aluminium foil
Pastry brush
Brushes for applying dough paste, paints and varnish
Water-based paints
Gloss polyurethane varnish

1 For the mould, cut a piece of cardboard 36 x 6cm (14 x 2½in). Divide and mark into four equal sections, each 9cm (3½in) long. Roll out dough to a thickness of about 1cm (⅜in). Using your cardboard strip as a template, cut out a dough oblong.

2. Cover the cardboard completely with aluminium foil. Bend the covered cardboard into its box-shape (don't worry about the base, you will make this at a later stage). Join the ends of the box with adhesive tape.

3 Working on the baking sheet, carefully press the dough onto the box, taking care not to distort its shape. Join the ends and seal them with dough paste. Smooth the surface of the dough with a damp (not wet) pastry brush.

4 Now model the shells by hand. Page 14 of the Materials and Techniques Section explains how in detail. Once you have made a selection of shells, arrange them on the box. Attach with dough paste.

5 Bake the box until it is hard enough to handle. Remove the foil mould from the inside. While it is still warm roll another piece of dough to a thickness of about 1cm (⅜in). Transfer the dough to your baking sheet and carefully place the shell box on top of it. Cut around the shell box so that the raw dough underneath becomes its base. (The warmth from the shell box should seal it to the base.) Put the box back in the oven to finish baking.

6 When the box is baked inside and out, remove from the oven and leave to cool. To paint, apply a thin wash of orange paint all over the box and shells. Highlight certain areas of the shells by dabbing on and rubbing in a tiny amount of black paint. Finally, varnish.

Style File

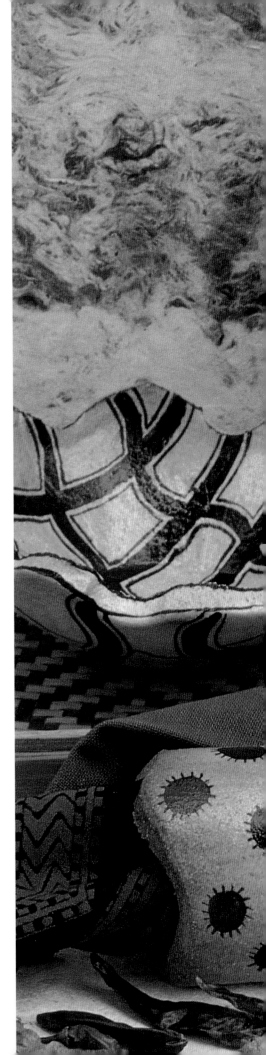

A nation's character and style are reflected in its craft work.
Some designs are handed down through generations of
model-makers, potters or needleworkers, while others are
simply modern interpretations of traditional themes.
Each project in this section uses salt dough to echo
the characteristics of traditional crafts. The merest hint of
ethnic patterning or colour is often all it takes to convey the
flavour of a design, so historical accuracy isn't important.
Vary shapes and paint finishes as much as you like. But do
try to keep surface decorations simple, for the most
effective results possible.

HOME-SWEET-HOME PLAQUE

Welcoming a friend or relative to their new home with a hand-made gift is a charming tradition. If you model this project with someone special in mind, the result couldn't be more personal. Simply cut out the plaque, attach the frame and then adapt the picture inside to suit the occasion. For example, you may prefer daisies to tulips – or why not model the house to look like the one your friend has moved into? A personal message could be painted in the space above the house.

Layers of relief work make this plaque quite thick, so tap-test your dough during baking to judge the cooking time. (For more information on baking, see pages 17–18.)

MATERIALS AND EQUIPMENT

Salt dough (see page 12)
Dough paste (see page 13)
Non-stick baking sheet
Ruler
Rolling pin
House and tulip templates (page 133)
Small kitchen knife
Small wooden spatula
Pastry brush
Brushes for applying dough paste, paints and varnish
1mm-thick wire, about 7cm (2¾in)
Wire cutters
Round-ended pliers
Water-based paints
Gloss polyurethane varnish

1 Roll out dough to a thickness of about 5mm (¼in). Cut out a rectangle of dough about 17 x 15 cm (6¾in x 6in). Make a frame by rolling four dough sausages (two 17cm (6¾in), two 15cm (6in). Attach them to the base shape with dough paste.

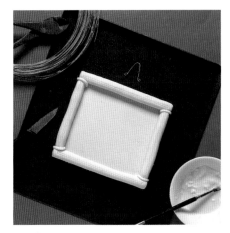

2 Roll thin sausages of dough and attach them over the corners of the dough frame. to disguise the joins in the frame. Score in the line detail on the frame. With the wire, make a hanging loop (see page 16). Embed this in the top of the plaque.

3 Roll out more dough to a thickness of about 5mm (¼in). Cut around the house template. Attach this shape centrally, about 3cm (1¼in) up from the lower part of the frame. Now cut out a door and two windows and attach to the house with dough paste. Score in the window detail. Roll a small ball of dough for the door knob and attach. Cut out fine strips of dough with a sharp knife and attach these to the roof. Score in fine, horizontal lines.

4 Cut around the templates to make five tulips from the rolled-out dough. Attach the tulips, about 1.5cm (⅝in) up from the bottom of the frame. Make stalks by cutting out short, narrow strips of dough. Attach with dough paste. Now model small leaves, score in veins and attach them in-between each tulip with dough paste. For the buds, roll small balls of dough, attach them between the tulips and make an indentation in each.

5 Add two leaves and a bud to the top left- and right-hand corners of the picture. Bake the plaque, remove from the oven and allow to cool. Paint the plaque using the finished photograph as a guide. Highlight the frame with a little gold paint, brushed on with quick strokes and a dry paint brush. When dry, varnish.

PATCHWORK FRAME

This frame is simple to make and easy to adapt to suit your own ideas. The surround has been scored to produce a patchwork effect and wire loops have been embedded in the back of the frame (to hold photographs or pictures in place). These loops must be flexible, so use thinner wire than the 1mm-type recommended for hanging loops – 30 amp fuse wire is ideal.

A hand-made finish gives home-produced patchwork its special appeal, so slight imperfections will add to this project's charm. If you prefer patterned patches, paint your own designs in all or some of the squares before varnishing. The finished frame should be simple and eye-catching – so stick to a few, carefully chosen colours for a truly traditional effect.

MATERIALS AND EQUIPMENT

Salt dough (see page 12)
Dough paste (see page 13)
Non-stick baking sheet
Ruler
Rolling pin
Frame template (page 134)
Small kitchen knife
Small wooden spatula
Brushes for applying dough paste, paints
and varnish
Pastry brush
1mm-thick wire, about 7cm (2¾in)
Flexible wire (fuse wire is ideal, about
12cm (4¾in)
Wire cutters
Round-ended pliers
Water-based paints
Gloss polyurethane varnish

1 Working straight onto baking sheet, roll out dough to a thickness of about 1cm (⅜in). Lay the frame template on top of the dough and cut around it with a sharp knife. Tidy any rough edges with a spatula or damp pastry brush.

2 Cut four pieces of flexible wire about 3cm (1¼in) long. Treat each piece of wire as though you were making a hanging loop (see page 16). Now embed the hooks in the back of the frame, position them according to the photograph. Make a hanging loop from the 7cm (2¾in) length of thicker wire. Embed it in the frame.

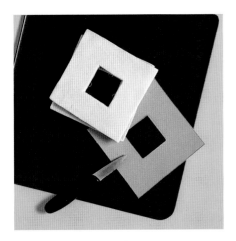

3 Half-bake the frame face down. Meanwhile, roll out more dough, this time to a thickness of about 5mm (¼in). Following step 1, cut out another frame. When the first frame is half-baked, take it from the oven. Carefully turn it over. Lay the raw dough on top of the half-baked frame. (The warmth from the lower frame should seal both pieces together.)

4 Seal all edges with dough paste, filling and smoothing any gaps as you go. Using a sharp knife, score in the patchwork squares and stitching detail. Return the frame to the oven and bake through. (See pages 17–18 for information on baking.) Paint, using the finished photograph as a guide. Varnish.

FOLK CANDLESTICKS

This project relies on simplicity for impact. Inspired by European folk-art, these hanging candlesticks put traditional design to practical use.

Just roll and coil three dough sausages by hand. Connect and flatten the shapes, then strengthen them with wire loops (these double-up as eyelets for a night-light stand). You could make the surface design more unique to you by painting it to suit your own taste and decor. If you decide to use your own colour scheme, bear in mind that bright patterns tend to contrast better with darker base shades. Choose a few, vivid colours for your pattern work and use a fine-bristle brush to produce a delicate finish.

Please don't use anything but a safety/night-light with this project. An ordinary candle may be unstable and could be a dangerous substitute.

MATERIALS AND EQUIPMENT

Salt dough (see page 12)
Dough paste (see page 13)
Non-stick baking sheet
Ruler
Rolling pin
Night-light stand template (page 134)
Small kitchen knife
Small wooden spatula
Brushes for applying dough paste, paints
and varnish
Pastry brush
1mm-thick wire, about 37cm (14½in)
Wire cutters
Round-ended pliers
Water-based paints
Gloss polyurethane varnish
Night-light

1 Working straight onto the baking sheet, by hand, roll a sausage of dough about 28cm (11in) long and about 2cm (³⁄₄in) thick. Roll two more sausages this time about 26cm (10¹⁄₄in) long and about 2cm (³⁄₄in) thick.

2 Bend the middle of the longest dough sausage into an inverted "U" shape. Roll the remaining tail pieces into coils. Bend the other two sausages into neatly coiled "S" shapes.

3 To join these three dough shapes together, press gently and seal with dough paste. With a rolling pin, roll over all the shapes lightly. Apply even pressure as you roll. Smooth the surface of the dough with a pastry brush.

4 Cut four pieces of wire, about 3cm (1¹⁄₄in) long. Treat each piece as though you were making a hanging loop (see page 16). Push the looped ends of the wire into the dough leaving about 1.5cm (¹⁄₂in) of each loop outside the dough. Make a hanging loop from 7cm (2³⁄₄in) of wire and embed it into the top of the dough.

5 Working straight onto the baking sheet, roll out dough to a thickness of about 1cm (³/₈in). Cut around your night-light stand template. Smooth and tidy any rough edges with a spatula. Press the night-light into the dough to make a small, raised lip around the base. (The indentation left by the night-light will eventually hold it in place.)

6 To decorate the stand, score a line around the raised lip with the point of your knife. Now score zigzags around the inner edge. Cut two 9cm (3½in) lengths of 1mm-thick wire and bend the ends into small loops. Keeping the night-light stand flat on the baking sheet, embed both wires about 3cm (1¼in) apart into the top of the stand.

7 To prepare the night-light stand for baking, scrunch up some foil to make a support for the two wires – this will stop them drooping in the oven. Bake the candlestick, remove from the oven and allow to cool. (For information on baking see pages 17–18.)

8 Paint the candlestick, using the photographs as a guide and then varnish. Attach the night-light stand to the base shape by pushing the wires through two inner loops of the base shape. Now bend the wires behind the base shape and fold them forward, to loop decoratively over the front of the candlestick.

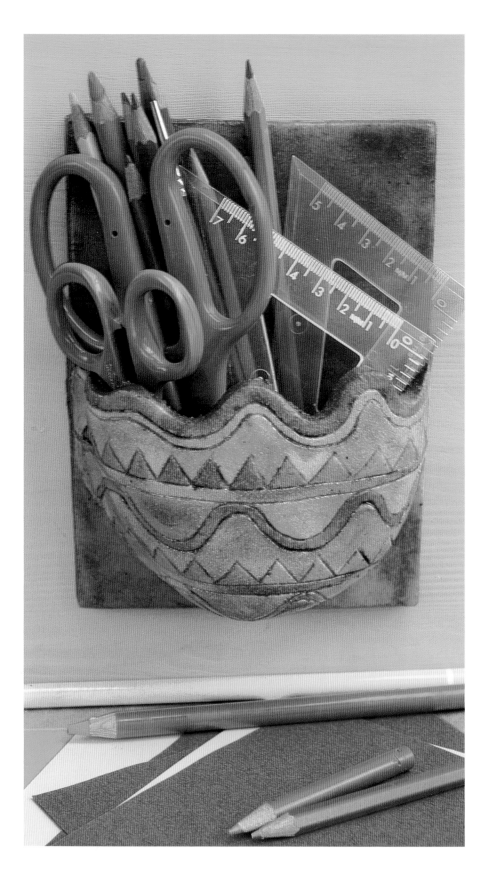

MEXICAN WALL BOWL

Washes of warm colour give this wall bowl a slightly faded, sun-soaked quality. To achieve this effect brush diluted paint over the base of the plaque in long, stroking movements, and then apply contrasting colours between the scored lines on the bowl. Unvarnished dough is extremely porous, so try not to overload your paint brush (too much diluted paint will seep down through the surface, soaking your model).

The bowl itself is moulded over a "pocket" of aluminium foil and you may find this technique useful for making other containers of different sizes. Just reduce or enlarge the dimensions to make smaller or larger bowls and either copy the decorative ideas used here, or reproduce colours and patterns from any number of traditional sources.

MATERIALS AND EQUIPMENT

Salt dough (see page 12)
Dough paste (see page 13)
Non-stick baking sheet
Ruler
Rolling pin
Template (page 134, optional)
Small kitchen knife
Small wooden spatula
Brushes for applying dough paste, paints and varnish
Pastry brush
Aluminium foil
Water-based paints
Gloss polyurethane varnish

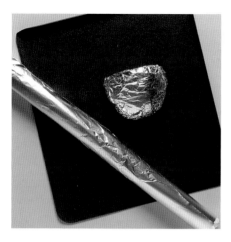

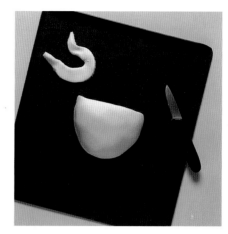

1 Make a mould for the bowl by shaping aluminium foil into a hollow, half-circle "pocket" about 12cm (4¾in) across and about 2.5cm (1in) high. The foil must be sturdy, so make it about 1cm (⅜in) thick.

2 Roll out dough to thickness of 1cm (⅜in). Cut out a rectangle, about 13 x 17cm (5 x 6¾in) or use the template. Tidy any rough edges with a spatula and smooth the surface with a damp pastry brush. Using the end of a paint brush, make a hanging hole at the top of the rectangle.

3 Roll out more dough to a thickness of 1cm (⅜in), carefully lay the dough over the foil "pocket" mould and trim away any excess.

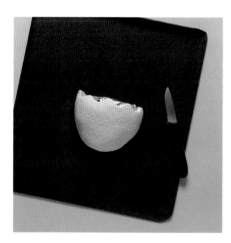

4 With a sharp knife, cut away the top of the bowl in a continuous, wavy line. Now add a surface pattern by scoring the dough with the point of your knife.

5 Bake the dough-covered mould and the rectangular piece of dough side by side on the same baking sheet. When the dough is half-baked (hard to touch and solid enough to handle without distortion), carefully remove the foil mould from the bowl. (For information on baking see pages 17–18.)

6 Taking advantage of the fact that both dough pieces are still warm, join them together. The heat from the bowl and rectangle should seal them together. Join any gaps between the pieces with thickened dough paste. Return to the oven to finish baking. When cool, paint your wall bowl. When the paint has dried, varnish.

ETHNIC BOWL AND NAPKIN RINGS

Make the most of the natural tones of baked dough by displaying the napkin rings and bowl (pictured opposite) on a wooden table or shelf, or against a stark, contrasting background. These projects have been baked to varying shades of brown and then decorated with a bold, but simple design. Both have fluted edges, created quite simply by cutting a wavy line into the raw dough. The salt dough bowl was moulded over a 15cm (6in) oven-proof bowl. If you would rather make a larger version, for fruit or pot-pourri, for example, use a bigger oven-proof bowl. The same instructions apply, no matter how large, or small a bowl you choose. The napkin rings are moulded over cardboard tubes. Be sure to cover each tube completely, inside and out, with foil. As long as you roll your dough out to an even thickness, join all seams securely and smooth any rough edges while the dough is still soft enough to handle, the end result should be neat, strong and very professional.

Although the napkin rings are painted to match the bowl, you may prefer a more personal finish. Either use other paint effects from this book (see pages 19–20 for more ideas), or how about reproducing the design on your favourite piece of crockery or table linen? If you are not confident enough to commit yourself to a more elaborate pattern, bake a plain tile of dough along with your napkin rings and use it as a practice piece.

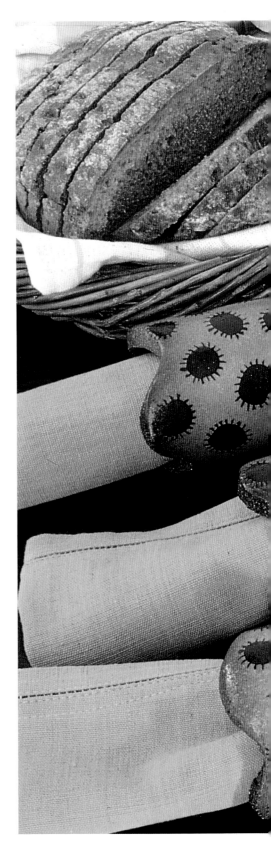

TO MAKE THE ETHNIC NAPKIN RING

MATERIALS AND EQUIPMENT

Salt dough (see page 12)
Dough paste (see page 13)
Non-stick baking sheet
Ruler
Rolling pin
Cardboard tube (to make the napkin ring,
about 4cm (1½in) in diameter)
Oven-proof bowl (to make the ethnic bowl)
Aluminium foil
Small kitchen knife
Small wooden spatula
Brushes for applying dough paste, paints
and varnish
Pastry brush
Water-based paint
Gloss polyurethane varnish

1 Cut the cardboard tube to a length of about 10cm (4in). Cover the tube, both inside and out with aluminium foil. Smooth the foil-covered surface until absolutely flat.

2 Roll out the dough to a thickness of about 1cm (³⁄₈in). Cut out a strip of dough about 5 x 22cm (2 x 8½in). Now cut a wavy line along either side of the dough strip.

3 Carefully wrap the dough strip around the middle of the foil mould. Leave about 2cm (¾in) of the mould jutting out at either end. Join the two ends of the dough strip. Cut off excess and trim and smooth any rough edges. Make sure that the join is well-sealed with dough paste and smoothed off neatly.

4 Stand the mould and ring upright on the baking sheet. Bake until the dough ring is hard to the touch (tap to test), and strong enough to handle without distorting its shape. (For more information on baking see pages 17–18.)

5 Remove the tube mould and return to the oven to finish baking. When the dough ring is fully baked, turn the oven to a higher setting and brown off in an upright position. Allow to cool completely. Paint (as for the ethnic bowl opposite) and varnish.

TO MAKE THE ETHNIC BOWL

1 Cover an oven-proof bowl with foil, taking care to smooth the surface and to tuck the ends over the edge of the bowl – about 5cm (2in) of the foil should over-lap inside the bowl. Roll out the dough to an even thickness of about 1cm (³⁄₈in). Carefully place the dough over the foil-covered bowl. Trim off any excess around the edges with a sharp knife. Take care not to cut into the foil.

2 Smooth the surface with a damp pastry brush. Cut a wavy line around the rim with a sharp knife. Take care not to cut into the foil. Smooth any rough edges with a damp paint brush and/or a spatula.

3 Half-bake the bowl, remove the foil covered mould and return to the oven, right-way-up, to finish baking. When the bowl is baked through, turn the oven tem-perature up and brown off.

4 When the bowl has baked to a rich brown, take it from the oven and allow to cool. Paint the pattern with black water-based paint, using the photograph as a guide. When dry, varnish.

MOULDED HEART

This heart has the same "sun-baked" finish as the ethnic bowl and napkin rings on pages 66–7. The flexibility of salt dough makes it ideal for moulding over foil. But, when using hand-made foil moulds, resist any temptation to smooth raw dough to perfection. The dappled gold colour produced by baking actually enhances slight surface flaws, and it would be a shame to lose this effect. When "browning off" in the oven keep an eye on your project. If the heart isn't baked enough, it will look pale and lifeless – too much, and it will become brittle and burnt. A boldly painted pattern contrasts beautifully with this natural background colour. Apply plenty of coats of varnish and your heart will look as if it has been baked under an African sun.

1 Working straight onto the baking sheet, roll out dough to about 1cm (³⁄₈in) thick. Lay the cardboard heart template on top of the dough and cut around the shape carefully.

2 Roll foil between your palms to make a ball. Flatten one side of the foil (to make a dome shape). This should measure about 10cm (4in) across the base and be about 3cm (1¹⁄₄in) high.

MATERIALS AND EQUIPMENT

Salt dough (see page 12)
Dough paste (see page 13)
Non-stick baking sheet
Ruler
Rolling pin
Heart template (page 137)
Aluminium foil
Small kitchen knife
Small wooden spatula
1mm-thick wire, about 7cm (2³⁄₄in)
Wire cutters
Round-ended pliers
Brushes for applying dough paste, paints
and varnish
Pastry brush
Water-based paint
Gloss polyurethane varnish

3 Place the foil dome on the baking sheet. Lift the dough heart and position it carefully over the dome. Pat and smooth the outer rim of the dough heart until it lies flat on the baking sheet, and tidy any rough edges with a spatula. Smooth the surface of your dough heart with a damp (not wet) pastry brush.

4 Make a hanging loop from the wire (see page 16) and embed the looped ends in the top of the heart, leaving about 5cm (2in) protruding outside the dough. Bake the heart until it is hard enough to handle. Remove the foil mould, and return to the oven to finish baking. Then turn the oven to a higher setting and brown off (see pages 17–18). When cool, paint (see the ethnic bowl on page 67) and varnish.

AFRICAN DOLLS

Threaded like puppets, and designed to slip and move on their wires, these African dolls almost come to life in your hands.

Although measurements are included in the instructions, they are just a rough guide to help you judge the doll's proportions. Don't worry if your dough shapes differ slightly from these measurements in length and width, but do try to keep their thicknesses a consistent 2cm (³⁄₄in), so that they all take the same amount of time to bake. You should bake the body sections to as natural-looking a finish as possible. Wait until each section blushes from pale tan to golden brown, then allow the dough to deepen to the shades you find most pleasing. The final moments of the browning off process are the most critical. When you are happy with the colour of your dough, take the body sections out of the oven immediately (if you hesitate, the dough could burn). Let each piece cool completely before painting and varnishing.

Detailed step-by-step instructions explain how to make the female doll. To make the male version (shown here and on page 75), follow steps 1 to 4 (leaving out obvious, anatomical differences). Thread one piece of wire through the upper half of the torso, crossways (as with the female doll), and another through the hip area of the torso. Then refer to the photograph to make the legs. Wire the legs separately, hooking them onto loops protruding from the ankle/foot sections. Finally, attach the legs to the hips of your doll.

TO MAKE THE FEMALE DOLL

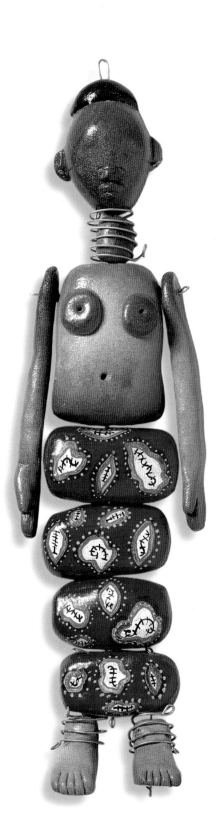

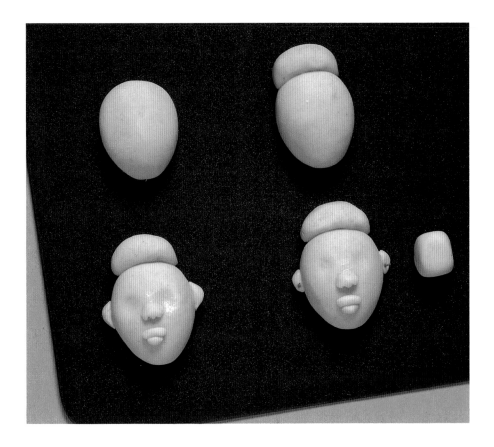

MATERIALS AND EQUIPMENT

Salt dough (see page 12)
Dough paste (see page 13)
Non-stick baking sheet
Ruler
Rolling pin
Small kitchen knife
Small wooden spatula
Brushes for applying dough paste, paints
and varnish
Pastry brush
1mm-thick wire, about 2m (2yd 6in)
Wire cutters
Round-ended pliers
Water-based paints
Gloss polyurethane varnish

1 To make the doll's head, roll an oval-shaped ball of dough by hand, about 4cm (1½in) long and 3.5cm (1⅜in) across. To make the hair, roll a smaller oval-shaped ball and attach it to the head with a little dough paste. Attach a small roll of dough to each side of the head and mould into ears. Add eye sockets by pressing lightly into the dough with your finger. For the mouth make two small, sausage shapes and attach with dough paste. Roll a small, triangular piece of dough for the nose. Attach and then pierce two small holes (for nostrils) with the point of a knife. Cut two 2cm (¾in) lengths of wire and push through ears (these will stay in during and after baking). The neck is a tube-shaped roll of dough, about 2cm (¾in) long and 1.5cm (⅝in) wide. Flatten the back of the head and neck by pressing them gently onto the baking sheet.

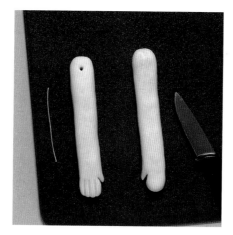

2 For the doll's torso, roll a thick sausage of dough. Pat gently into a squarer shape, about 7 x 5cm (2¾ x 2in), keeping the surface and edges natural-looking and the back flat. Squeeze the dough to shape a waist. Flatten two balls of dough for breasts – attach with dough paste. Indent each one with the end of some wire and make a third indentation in the stomach.

3 To make the arms, roll two sausages about 12cm (4¾in) long. Flatten the undersides. Squash the end of each arm into a paddle shape. Score lines to make fingers and thumbs with a knife. Trim the end of the thumbs to make them shorter than the fingers. Make holes at the top of the arms with a piece of wire (make sure that they don't close up when baking).

4 Taking care not to distort the dough, guide a piece of wire through the head, neck and torso. The wire should pass through the dough shape, with about 2cm (¾in) jutting out at either end. Now guide a piece of wire through the top half of the torso, horizontally (this wire stays in place after baking). The two pieces of torso wire must not touch inside the dough shape.

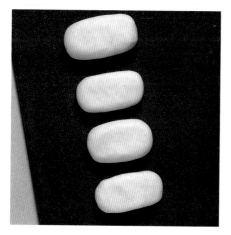

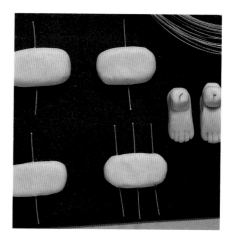

5 To make the lower half of the doll, roll a thick sausage of dough. Pat into an oblong with rounded edges – the finished piece should be about 6cm (2⅜in) long and 3cm (1¼in) wide. Now make three more similar, but shorter pieces about 5cm (2in) long and 3cm (1¼in) wide. All dough pieces should have flat backs.

6 To make the feet, roll two short sausages of dough (about 4cm (1½in) long). Press down on the front of each piece with your thumb and gently mould into a foot about 2cm (¾in) across. Attach two small pieces of dough for the ankles with dough paste Make sure that the soles are flat. Score lines to mark the toes.

7 Guide a length of wire through the middle of each of the four lower-body (sarong) sections. Now pass two more pieces of wire through the bottom sarong piece (the feet will be threaded to this piece). Leave about 2cm (¾in) of wire at either end. Also, guide a piece of wire down through the centre of each ankle.

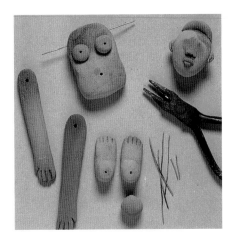

8 Bake the dough pieces in the oven. Turn all the wires regularly to prevent the holes closing up. Keep a close eye on the dough shapes (checking that the smaller ones don't burn). When the four lower-body sections are cooked, remove from the oven and allow to cool. Leave the other pieces in the oven and brown off. Paint the four lower-body parts.

9 Check the browning process carefully. The pieces should brown unevenly (to produce natural-looking skin-tones) without burning. When your dough shapes are cool, withdraw all wires except the one running across the torso. Pull the wires out very gently, using your pliers.

10 Paint the hair black and allow to dry. Varnish the painted (sarong) pieces, the head and the rest of the browned off dough shapes and leave all parts of the doll to dry.

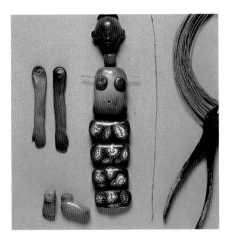

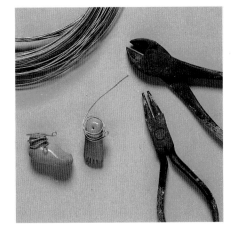

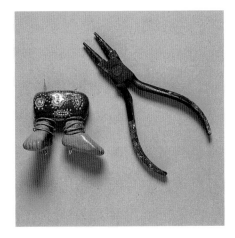

11 Calculate the length of wire needed to thread your doll by arranging the dough pieces in order. Cut enough wire to pass through the lower-body (sarong), torso, neck and head, about 35cm (13¾in). The wire should be long enough to pass through the dough pieces with about 1.5cm (⅝in) excess at either end.

12 Make ankle bracelets by cutting enough wire to wrap around each ankle four or five times – two lengths of about 25cm (10in). Using the round-ended pliers, coil the wire around each ankle and loop ends to neaten.

13 Thread the feet to the bottom sarong piece with two lengths of wire. Guide one piece of wire up through the left foot and through the hole in the left side of the bottom sarong piece (with ankle bracelet in place). Thread the right foot to the right side of the sarong in the same way. Make locking loops at each end of wire.

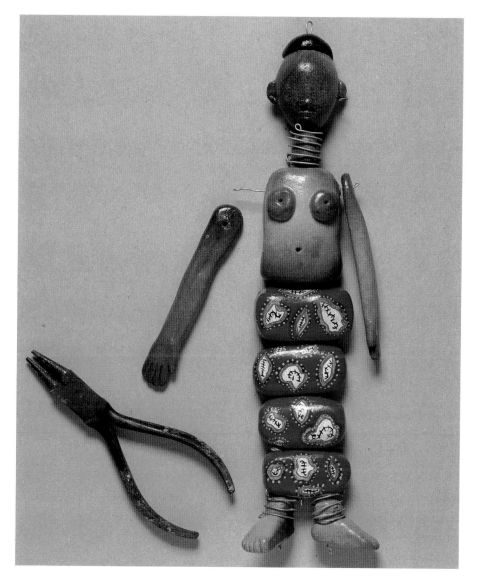

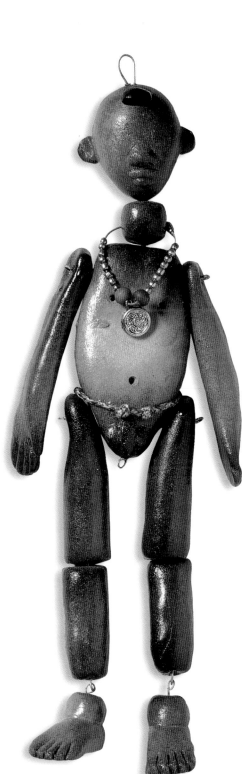

14 Make a necklace by cutting enough wire to wrap around the neck five or six times – about 35cm (13¾in). Coil wire around the neck and loop ends to neaten. Finish threading by guiding a wire up through the remaining hole in the bottom sarong piece, through the other three sarong pieces, torso, neck and head. Leave room for movement between pieces, and bend a small, locking loop at either end of the wire. Attach arms by threading them onto wire ends (jutting out from upper torso). Bend locking loops to finish.

The male doll is modelled in the same way as the female (see page 71). Don't thread your doll too tightly – the dough pieces should slip slightly on the wires to allow for movement.

Feasts and Festivals

At Easter, Christmas, Thanksgiving and Halloween
– whether you're marking the occasion with a small family
gathering, or throwing a bigger party for neighbours and
friends – decorations with specific themes add originality
and style to traditional celebrations.

The projects in this section are inspired by particular
festivals. But they are just as effective in everyday
surroundings – especially if you adapt them to suit your
own taste and decor. Make a big impression by modelling a
whole set of decorations, or choose one salt dough piece
from a group of projects. Even the tiniest touch of
inspiration can add something special to a room.

THE EASTER TABLE

This Easter table's centrepiece is a hen bowl, modelled in two halves. One half is a lattice-work nest, while the other is moulded in one piece and uses relief-work and surface scoring to make the feathered head, wings and tail. The hen bowl is perfect for storing Easter surprises. Hand-painted (or wrapped chocolate) eggs, small gifts for children and home-made cookies are all ideal festive treats. Or why not hide a whole family of tiny Easter chicks inside?

To make Easter chicks, just roll small lumps of salt dough into thick sausage shapes. Press them onto a flat surface to make their bases firm and squeeze each dough piece into shape with your thumb and forefinger. Then, using the photograph to guide you, make small indentations for the eyes. Model tiny beaks and attach a small ball of dough above each one. After baking, paint your chicks a sunny yellow, leave their beaks a natural dough-colour for contrast, then varnish as usual.

The Easter theme continues with the simplest of napkin rings. Shaped like chicks, and painted a radiant yellow, these double-up cleverly as egg-cup stands. Make one for each guest and arrange them around the hen centrepiece to add splashes of Spring colour to your table.

Moulded egg-cups with cut-away rims create an exotic finishing touch. Paint them in rich colours, brush a swirl of gold inside each one and your festive setting is complete.

TO MAKE THE HEN LID

MATERIALS AND EQUIPMENT
Salt dough (see page 12)
Dough paste (see page 13)
Non-stick baking sheet
Ruler
Rolling pin
Wing template (page 135)
Small kitchen knife
Small wooden spatula
Oven-proof bowl
Aluminium foil
Wire for indenting detail
Pastry brush
Brushes for applying dough paste, paints and varnish
Water-based paints
Gloss polyurethane varnish

1 Cover an oven-proof bowl with foil, taking care to smooth the surface. About 5cm (2in) of the foil should overlap inside the bowl. Roll out dough to an even thickness of about 1cm (³⁄₈in). Place the dough over the foil-covered bowl. Trim away excess dough with a sharp knife. Smooth the surface with a damp pastry brush. Tidy any rough edges with a spatula.

2 For the head and neck, roll a horn-shaped piece of dough about 7cm (2³⁄₄in) long, 5cm (2in) across, tapering to about 1cm (³⁄₈in). Position this shape at the "front", about 3cm (1¹⁄₄in) up from the rim. Attach with dough paste and mould into a head and neck. For the head-comb, roll three balls of dough, flatten the bases and squeeze into wedges. Attach in a row.

3 The feathers are balls of dough, flattened into petal shapes. Arrange the largest feathers, about 1.5cm (⁵⁄₈in) long and 1cm (³⁄₈in) wide, around the base of the neck. Overlap the feathers and make them smaller as you move toward the head. Score lines down each feather. Tease the tips of some of the feathers upward.

4 Indent eye sockets with the end of a paint brush. In the centre, attach balls of dough with dough paste. Indent each ball with wire. The cheek flaps and beak are cones of dough. Flatten their bases and attach to the face. Make the beak pointed and score in a line to define the two halves. Attach a ball of dough above the beak.

5 To make the tail, roll a thick wedge-shaped sausage of dough about 5cm (2in) long. Attach to the back of the hen with dough paste. Disguise the join at the base of the tail with a single layer of feathers (the same type as you used for the head and neck). They should fan out around the tail on the dough base.

6 The tail feathers are long, petal-shaped pieces of dough. Squeeze the tips into points and vary the lengths – about 1.5–3cm (⅝in–1¼in). First, attach the shorter feathers in layers up the back of the tail with dough paste. Next attach the longer feathers up each side and the front of the tail. Now score lines on each feather with the point of your knife.

7 Roll out dough to a thickness of about 5mm (¼in). Cut around template to make wings. Attach with dough paste. Using the photograph of the finished hen as a guide, score in feather patterns. Bake in the oven until the dough is hard enough to handle without distorting, take it from the oven. Carefully remove the oven-proof bowl, and peel the foil away from the inside. Return the hen lid back to the oven to finish baking. (For more information on baking see pages 17–18.)

8 When cool, brush a wash of dark brown paint over your hen. Do not paint the head-comb, eyeballs, cheek flaps and beak. Use a small brush to dab a tiny amount of black paint onto the ends of some of the larger feathers and wings, rub in with your finger or a soft rag. Paint the remaining features in bright colours.

TO MAKE THE HEN'S NEST

MATERIALS AND EQUIPMENT

Salt dough (see page 12)
Dough paste (see page 13)
Non-stick baking sheet
Ruler
Rolling pin
Small kitchen knife
Small wooden spatula
Oven-proof bowl
Aluminium foil
Pizza cutter or a long-bladed knife for
cutting strips of dough
Brushes for applying dough paste, paints
and varnish
Water-based paint
Gloss polyurethane varnish

1 Cover an oven-proof bowl with foil. Roll out dough to an even thickness of 5mm (¼in). Using a pizza cutter or long-bladed knife, cut strips of dough a little longer than the upside-down bowl and about 1.5cm (⅝in) wide. Start by positioning a cross of two strips in the centre of the mould. Now add more strips, weaving them over and under.

2 When the bowl is covered in woven strips, trim excess dough away from the rim. Gently squeeze the overlapping pieces at the edge so that they stick neatly together. Cut a strip of dough long enough to go around the rim of the bowl. Press gently to attach. Apply a little dough paste before attaching, if necessary.

3 Roll thin sausages of dough into coils and flatten them with your finger. Using the photograph as a guide, attach the decorative coils with dough paste. With a rolling pin, gently flatten the middle of your lattice work as this will be the base.

4 Bake the nest, face down on its mould. When the nest is hard enough to handle without distorting, take it from the oven. Remove the oven-proof bowl and carefully peel away the tin foil. (For more information on baking see pages 17–18.)

5 Return the nest to the oven (right-way-up) until it's baked through. To deepen the natural colour, turn the oven to a higher setting and, keeping a close eye on the dough nest, brown off. When cool, paint the coils yellow and then varnish.

Templates are provided for the napkin rings and egg cups pictured here, but the two small chicks are modelled by hand. Simply squeeze balls of dough into shape, add indentations for eyes and attach tiny, cone-shaped beaks. After baking, paint the chicks a sunny yellow.

TO MAKE THE CHICK NAPKIN RING

MATERIALS AND EQUIPMENT

Salt dough (see page 12)
Dough paste (see page 13)
Non-stick baking sheet
Rolling pin
Chick napkin ring template (page 135)
Small kitchen knife
Small wooden spatula
Pastry brush
Wire for indenting detail
Brushes for applying dough paste, paints
and varnish
Water-based paint
Gloss polyurethane varnish

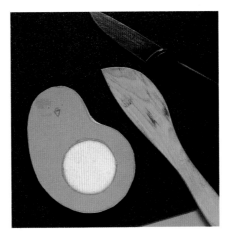

1 Roll out dough to a thickness of 1cm (³⁄₈in). Place the template on top of the dough and cut around it with a sharp kitchen knife. Smooth any rough edges with a damp paint brush, a small spatula or the flat side of your knife.

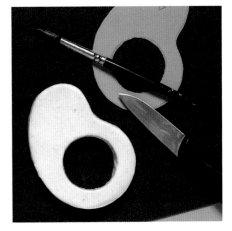

2 Cut out the circle in the middle of the template. Smooth any rough edges with a damp paint brush.

3 Using your knife, score simple feather details on the top of the chick's head. Add eyes by making small indentations with the end of a piece of wire. The beak is a tiny heart-shaped piece of dough attached to an even smaller ball of dough. Attach beak pieces with a little dough paste.

4 Bake, allow to cool. (For more information on baking see pages 17–18.) Paint the napkin ring bright yellow, leaving the chick's beak its natural dough-colour. Allow to dry and then varnish.

TO MAKE THE EGG CUP

MATERIALS AND EQUIPMENT

Salt dough (see page 12)
Dough paste (see page 13)
Non-stick baking sheet
Rolling pin
Egg cup template (page 135)
Small kitchen knife
Small wooden spatula
Hard-boiled egg(s)
Oven-proof egg cup(s)
Aluminium foil
Pastry brush
Brushes for applying dough paste, paints and varnish
Water-based paints
Gloss polyurethane varnish

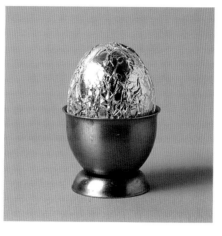

1 Cover a hard-boiled egg with foil, making sure that the surface is smooth. Place the foil-covered egg in an oven-proof egg cup.

2 Roll out dough to a thickness of 5mm (¼in). Cut around circular template. Now place the circle of dough centrally over your foil-covered egg. Smooth the surface with a damp pastry brush.

3 Using the photograph as a guide, cut a serrated edge into the rim of the dough, take care not to cut into the foil. Make a flat base for your dough egg cup to stand on by flattening the top of the dough with a spatula. Bake (see pages 17–18 for information on baking).

4 When the dough is hard enough to handle, take it out of the oven. Now lift the foil-covered egg and the dough out of the egg cup. Carefully remove the foil-covered egg and turn your dough egg cup the right way up. Return it to the oven to finish baking.

5 When baked, allow to cool – then paint, using the photograph as a guide, and finally, varnish.

CHRISTMAS DECORATIONS

No matter how exclusive they may be, shop-bought decorations can never match the originality and charm of home-made designs.

Cherubs and celestial horns make stunning tree trimmings. Either paint them in bright, solid colours (deep red, burnished gold, silver and purple contrast beautifully with the green of a Christmas tree), or use the special effects pictured here. The cherub and celestial horn were covered in washes of colour and then brushed with gold to create shimmering highlights.

The small holly wreath does not take long to model, so cut out and decorate as many as you can bake at one time. When you have painted your decorations, apply layers of gloss varnish to make them glisten under the lights of the Christmas tree.

A large wreath, loaded with fruit, berries and nuts is the most traditional of dough craft designs. Although the relief-work is very easy to model and attach, avoid making too many shapes at one time. Cover any prepared leaves and fruits with a damp cloth (to prevent drying) until you are ready to arrange them onto the base shape. You could reduce the size of the wreath by rolling out a smaller oval of dough for the base shape (see step 1, page 92). But working on too small a scale can be fiddly – and it would be a shame to lose the opulence and splendour of the fully sized version of this design.

TO MAKE THE HOLLY WREATH

MATERIALS AND EQUIPMENT

Salt dough (see page 12)
Dough paste (see page 13)
Non-stick baking sheet
Rolling pin
Small kitchen knife
Small wooden spatula
Two lids, glasses or pastry cutters, one about
3cm (1¼in) larger than the other
Brushes for applying dough paste, paints
and varnish
Water-based paints
Gloss polyurethane varnish
Festive ribbon

1 Roll out dough to a thickness of 5mm (¼in). Use the larger lid (glass or pastry cutter) to stamp out a circle in the dough. Then press out an inner circle with the smaller lid (glass or cookie cutter).

2 Flatten small balls of dough and shape them into leaves. Score in veins. Roll small balls of dough to make berries.

3 Attach the leaves and berries to your dough wreath with a little dough paste.

4 Bake, and allow to cool. (For information on baking see pages 17–18.) Paint using green for the leaves, red for the berries and brush on gold highlights. When dry, varnish. Thread with festive ribbon to hang.

TO MAKE THE CHERUB

MATERIALS AND EQUIPMENT

Salt dough (see page 12)
Dough paste (see page 13)
Non-stick baking sheet
Ruler
Small kitchen knife
Small wooden spatula
1mm-thick wire, about 7cm (2¹⁄₄in)
*Brushes for applying dough paste, paints
and varnish*
Water-based paints
Gloss polyurethane varnish

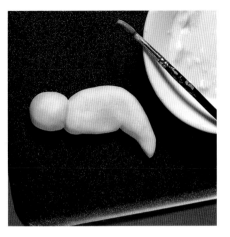

1 Roll a sausage of dough about 7cm
(2³⁄₄in) long. Model it into a body and leg
shape, about 1cm (³⁄₈in) thick. Roll a ball
for the head. Flatten it gently until the
dough is about 1cm (³⁄₈in) thick. Attach
the head to the body with dough paste.

2 Flatten and shape a sausage of dough,
about 3cm (1¹⁄₄in) long, into a second leg.
Shape a sausage of dough 4cm (1¹⁄₂in) long
into an arm. Flatten a ball of dough into a
petal-shaped wing. Attach the leg, arm
and wing with dough paste. Score in lines.

3 Roll a sausage for the second arm,
about 4cm (1¹⁄₂in) long, 1cm (³⁄₈in) thick.
Attach it across the cherub with dough
paste. For the hair, roll small sausages,
twist each sausage and attach to the head.
Make a hanging loop from the wire (see
page 16). Embed it just below the wing.

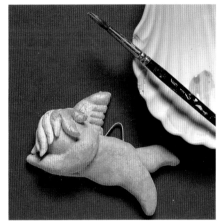

4 Bake (see pages 17–18 for information
on baking). When the cherub is cool,
apply a wash of flesh-coloured paint to the
body. Paint the hair and the wing gold.
Lightly brush gold paint over the body to
add highlights. Varnish.

TO MAKE THE CELESTIAL HORN

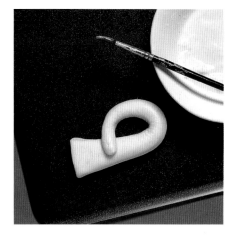

MATERIALS AND EQUIPMENT

Salt dough (see page 12)
Dough paste (see page 13)
Non-stick baking sheet
Ruler
Small kitchen knife
Small wooden spatula
Brushes for applying dough paste, paints
and varnish
Water-based paints
Gloss polyurethane varnish
Festive ribbon

1 Working straight onto the baking sheet, roll a long sausage of dough, about 17cm (6½in) long and 1.5cm (⅝in) thick. Flatten one end of the sausage to form the horn's bell. Roll the other end into a point.

2 Curl the dough into a horn shape and secure the end with dough paste.

3 Roll three small balls and attach them with dough paste. Make a larger ball and attach it to the horn as a mouthpiece.

4 Bake (see pages 17–18 for information on baking). When cool, cover the horn with a wash of orange paint. Brush on gold paint to highlight. When the paint is dry, varnish. Thread with festive ribbon to hang.

TO MAKE THE CHRISTMAS WREATH

MATERIALS AND EQUIPMENT

Salt dough (see page 12)
Dough paste (see page 13)
Non-stick baking sheet
Rolling pin
Leaf and wreath templates (pages 131 and 135)
Small kitchen knife
Small wooden spatula
Dried cloves
Brushes for applying dough paste, paints and varnish
Rag or paper towel to apply paint finishes
Water-based paints
Gloss polyurethane varnish

1 Working straight onto the baking sheet, roll out dough to a thickness of 1cm (³⁄₈in). Lay the template on the dough and cut around it to make the base of the wreath. Smooth any rough edges with damp brush or a spatula.

2 Roll out dough to a thickness of 5mm (¹⁄₄in). Cut around the leaf template, tidy any rough edges with a spatula. Score in veins. Only make as many leaves as you can attach before the dough dries out. Arrange leaves at an angle, creating an even border around the wreath. Bend the leaves slightly, so they overlap the edges of the base shape. Attach with dough paste.

3 To make pears, roll balls of dough by hand, model them into pear-shapes. Push a dried clove "flower" into the bottom of each pear and a dried clove stalk into the top. To make plums, roll smaller balls of dough. Squeeze the ends into points. Attach with dough paste.

4 To make apples and oranges, roll balls of dough by hand. Push a dried clove stalk into the top of each dough apple. Push a dried clove flower into the top of each dough orange. Attach with dough paste.

5 To make grapes, berries and nuts, roll small balls of dough by hand. Attach the grapes to your wreath in long bunches. Attach the berries to the wreath in groups. Indent the centre of each berry with the end of a paint brush. Attach the nuts to your wreath in groups. Use dough paste to attach the grapes, berries and nuts.

6 To make small leaves, flatten small balls of dough and shape them into leaves. Score in veins. Position three leaves above the grapes, as in the photograph. Attach these small leaves with dough paste. Use them to fill gaps in the arrangement, tucking them under the edges of fruits to make the overall effect thick and lush.

7 Bake the wreath (see pages 17–18 for information on baking). When it has cooled completely, paint the wreath. To make the outer leaves rich and festive, paint them green and dab on brown paint for contrast.

8 Paint the fruits with a base wash in their natural colours, dabbing on darker tones for contrast. Paint the smaller leaves bright green. When the paint is dry, use an almost-dry paint brush (wipe excess paint off the bristles) to brush on gold paint sparingly over the outside leaves. Varnish.

WHEAT PLAQUE

Highly decorative and particularly traditional, this project is also very simple to make. The custom of fashioning wheat sheaves from bread dough is hundreds of years old, but because this dough contains salt, it will be more durable than most edible bread mixtures. Varnishing deepens the golden tones of baked dough and provides a protective seal, which should prolong the life of your plaque still further.

Take advantage of this project's simplicity by leaving the baked dough its natural colour. Once you have covered the basic plaque shape with layers of wheat and a sprinkling of cornflowers, the only highlights necessary are a touch of blue for the cornflowers and a subtle brush of yellow on the ears of wheat.

MATERIALS AND EQUIPMENT

Salt dough (see page 12)
Dough paste (see page 13)
Non-stick baking sheet
Ruler
Rolling pin
Wheat plaque template (page 136)
Small kitchen knife
Small wooden spatula
1mm-thick wire, about 7cm (2¾in)
Wire cutters
Round-ended pliers
Garlic press
Brushes for applying dough paste, paints and varnish
Water-based paints
Gloss polyurethane varnish
String or natural-coloured raffia for decoration

1 Working straight onto the baking sheet, roll out dough to thickness of 1cm (⅜in). Cut around the wheat template. Tidy any rough edges with a spatula. Make a hanging loop from the wire (see page 16). Embed the hanging loop in the top of the dough shape.

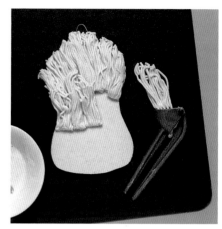

2 Squeeze dough through a garlic press. Brush a small amount of dough paste directly onto the base and then lay each bunch of strands onto the base shape. Starting from the top, work your way down the base shape in layers, overlapping the ends of the dough strands as you go.

3 To make ears of wheat, model small leaf-shapes by hand. Score in lines with the point of a knife. Attach the ears of wheat to the top half of the plaque with dough paste (use the photograph as a guide, or create your own arrangement).

4 To make cornflowers, roll balls of dough by hand. Attach to the plaque with dough paste. Using the end of a paint brush, indent the centre of each ball. Now make petal shapes by scoring lines around the indentation. Bake the plaque (tap to test). Turn the oven to a higher setting and brown off for a natural effect. (For more information on baking see pages 17–18.)

5 Leave the plaque its natural, baked colour, but add touches of blue by painting the cornflowers. Dip a dry brush into some yellow paint (wipe off excess) and brush lightly over the ears of wheat. Tie string or natural-coloured raffia around the middle to decorate.

HORN OF PLENTY

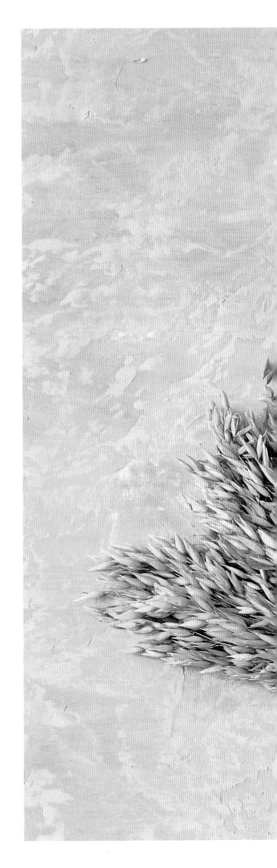

Whether you use it as a wall bowl or as the centrepiece for a festive table – a horn of plenty makes a beautiful and practical decoration.

This model is made up of two simple shapes – a flat, rectangular plaque and a long, curved bowl – which are joined together and trimmed to fit. It is decorated with coils, ropes and studs.

Aluminium foil is used for the mould because it is a very versatile and flexible material. A good mould should be strong enough to support the dough throughout baking, so scrunch the foil into a firm, compact wad. Bend the wad into a horn shape and then drape your dough over it.

The instructions include measurements, but don't worry about small variations in size. If you use your own foil mould as a guide, the finished horn should stay in proportion, even if its dimensions differ slightly from those supplied here.

MATERIALS AND EQUIPMENT

Salt dough (see page 12)
Dough paste (see page 13)
Non-stick baking sheet
Ruler
Rolling pin
Small kitchen knife
Small wooden spatula
Aluminium foil
Brushes for applying dough paste, paints
and varnish
Water-based paints
Gloss polyurethane varnish

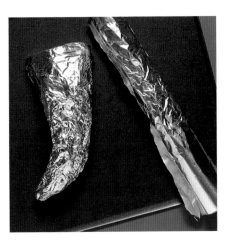

1 Working straight onto the baking sheet, first make a mould for the dough. Do this by scrunching aluminium foil into a hollow, horn-shaped pocket. The mould should be about 30cm (11³⁄₄in) long, about 20cm (8in) wide at its widest point, and about 6cm (2³⁄₈in) high.

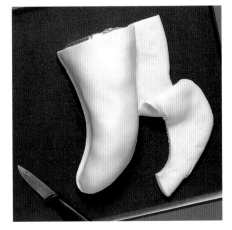

2 Roll out dough to a thickness of about 1cm (³⁄₈in). Drape the dough over the foil mould and gently squeeze it into shape. Trim off any excess dough and smooth any rough edges.

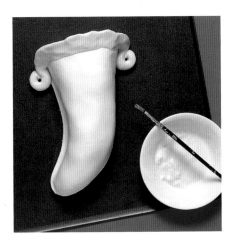

3 Roll a sausage of dough, about 6cm (2³⁄₈in) longer than the opening of the horn. Attach this around the opening with dough paste, leaving 3cm (1¹⁄₄in) trailing on either side. Squeeze the sausage between your thumb and forefinger to produce a wavy effect. Roll the tails of the sausage inward to form coils. Push a hole through each coil with the end of a paint brush.

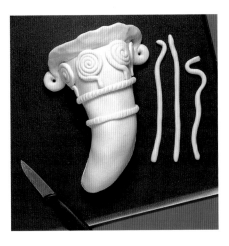

4 The coils are simply hand-rolled sausages of dough. Coil them into spirals, leaving short, decorative tail-pieces curling downward. Arrange and attach them around the top section of the horn with dough paste. Make decorative ropes by rolling thin sausages of dough by hand. Attach them at intervals across the horn and score in lines to produce a rope effect.

5 Make decorative studs by rolling small balls of dough. Flatten the balls, attach them to the horn with dough paste and then indent each one with the end of a paint brush. Half-bake the horn until it is hard enough to handle without distorting, and then carefully remove the foil mould. (For more information on baking see pages 17–18.)

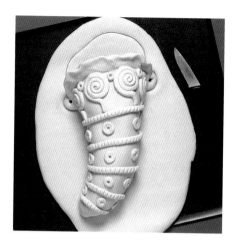

6 Roll out dough to an even thickness of 1cm (³⁄₈in). The dough should be wider than the horn and about 5cm (2in) longer at the top. Press the half-baked horn onto the dough. Cut around the horn and shape the raw dough at the top into a half-circle. Re-pierce the side holes. The warmth of the horn should seal it to the dough base.

7 Add a trimming to the top of the half-circle by attaching a hand-rolled sausage of dough and scoring in a rope effect. Pierce a hanging hole through the top of the base with end of paint brush. Now trim off excess dough and fill any gaps between the horn and its new base with thickened dough paste.

8 Put the horn back in the oven to bake through. When it's cool, paint your horn of plenty in rich, vibrant colours, using the photographs as a guide. Varnish when the paint is dry.

PUMPKIN PLAQUE

Although this pumpkin plaque is a perfect Halloween decoration, the various, soft greens of its leaves and the subtle orange washes of the pumpkin itself also make it a beautiful year-round ornament. The pumpkin is simply made from lengths of hand-rolled dough, moulded over a foil dome. The two longest rolls extend outward and coil up at the ends to provide a base for the leaves and vine tails. Because it will eventually hang on a wall, the back of the pumpkin plaque should be as flat as possible. So, work straight onto your baking sheet and gently press any smaller shapes (like the tips of overhanging leaves) onto the surface to keep their backs level. Use a damp pastry brush to smooth and blend the sections of the pumpkin into place.

For more information on modelling leaves see the Materials and Techniques section, page 15.

MATERIALS AND EQUIPMENT

Salt dough (see page 12)
Dough paste (see page 13)
Non-stick baking sheet
Ruler
Rolling pin
Vine leaf template (page 130)
Small kitchen knife
Small wooden spatula
Aluminium foil
1mm-thick wire, about 7cm (2¼in)
Wire cutters
Round-ended pliers
Brushes for applying dough paste, paints and varnish
Rag or paper towel to apply paint finishes
Water-based paints
Gloss polyurethane varnish

1 Working straight onto the baking sheet, roll some aluminium foil into a ball and press it down on the baking sheet to flatten its base. You should now have a dome of foil, measuring about 3cm (1¼in) high and 9cm (3½in) across the base.

2 Roll a long sausage of dough about 66cm (26in) long and about 2cm (¾in) thick. Place the foil dome against the central point of the sausage. Bend the dough around the foil dome. Join together at the top of the dome, applying a little dough paste. Make sure that the "tails" of dough left over are equal in length. Now coil the tails, using the photograph as a guide.

3 Gently flatten the coiled tail pieces with the palm of your hand. Using the 7cm (2¾in) length of wire, make a hanging loop (see page 16). Embed the ends of the loop in the top of the plaque.

4 Roll six dough sausages – about 15cm (6in) long and about 1.5cm (½in) wide. Gently squeeze the ends of each sausage into a point. Now lay the dough sausages over the foil mould. When the mould is covered, fill and seal any gaps with thickened dough paste. Smooth any untidy edges at the top and base of the pumpkin.

5 Mould a small sausage of dough into a stalk shape. Squeeze the end into a point. Attach with dough paste. Roll out dough to a thickness of 5mm (¼in). Using the vine leaf template, cut out six leaves. Score in veins with the point of a knife. Overlap some of the leaves, bend the ends slightly and attach with dough paste.

6 Roll three very thin sausages. Allow them to fall into waved shapes as you drape them across the leaves. Secure with dough paste. Half-bake the plaque, remove the foil mould and return to the oven to finish baking. (For more information on baking see pages 17–18.) Paint the pumpkin plaque. When dry, varnish.

Special Occasions

Whether you are celebrating the birth of a baby, an
anniversary, a wedding, or simply celebrating for the sake
of it, a special occasion is a perfect excuse to be creative.
Home-made gifts and decorations transform anniversaries
and celebrations into memorable occasions, especially when
they are designed with someone special in mind.
This section should encourage you to indulge your natural
sense of colour and style. If you don't have the confidence to
use the projects as patterns for your own designs, add a
touch of individuality by making smaller changes in colour
or surface pattern, for example.

VALENTINE HEARTS

The heart is a charming romantic symbol and its shape is extremely rewarding to decorate. Relief work and uncomplicated paint effects can turn the simplest of salt dough shapes into something special within minutes. This group of projects shows you just how adaptable a single moulded heart design can be.

Compact in size and very simple to make, the small Heart of Gold on this page is a good starting point. It uses exactly the same, basic moulding technique as the larger hearts pictured opposite, but only needs a wash of colour and some burnished highlights as decoration.

Just like the small gold heart, the larger hearts are simply raw dough shapes, draped and trimmed over a foil dome. The instructions show you how a little flair and ingenuity can give each one a very distinctive finish.

The Coiled and Swirled Hearts are edged with hand-rolled decoration. Bright, contrasting colours are used to emphasize this relief work on the Coiled Heart, but in the case of the Swirled Heart, a rub-off paint effect produces a deep bronze sheen, surrounding a pattern on the raised centre. The Cut-Out Heart's uncluttered lines and surface scoring provide its impact. A sharp, clean zigzag design in darker paint creates an eye-catching frame for the inner cut-out shape. The dramatic Cupid's Arrow Heart is pierced before baking. When the heart has been painted and varnished, an arrow of twisted wire is threaded through the holes.

MATERIALS AND EQUIPMENT

Salt dough (see page 12)
Dough paste (see page 13)
Non-stick baking sheet
Ruler
Rolling pin
Heart of Gold template (page 136)
Small kitchen knife
Small wooden spatula
Aluminium foil
Brushes for applying dough paste, paints and varnish
Pastry brush
Fish slice
1mm-thick wire, about 7cm (2¼in)
Wire cutters
Round-ended pliers
Rag or paper towel to apply paint finishes
Water-based paints
Gloss polyurethane varnish

1 Working straight onto your baking sheet, roll out dough to an even thickness of about 1cm (⅜in). Lay the heart template on top of the dough and cut around the shape carefully. Roll some foil between your palms to make a ball. Flatten one side of the foil to make a dome shape. This should measure about 6.5cm (2½in) across the base and be about 2.5cm (1in) high.

2 Using a fish slice (to avoid distorting the dough), lay the heart over the dome. Pat and smooth the outer rim of the dough heart until it lies flat. Smooth the surface with a damp pastry brush and tidy any rough edges with a spatula. Make a hanging loop from the wire (see page 16). Embed the loop into the top of the heart.

3 Half-bake the heart. remove the foil mould and return to the oven to finish baking (see pages 17–18). Allow to cool, then apply an even layer of black paint. Let this dry. Dip a soft rag into a tiny amount of gold paint and dab this onto the black surface colour to produce an antique-type finish. When dry, varnish.

TO MAKE THE COILED HEART

For the Coiled and Swirled Hearts, follow steps 1–2 of Heart of Gold (see page 104). The foil dome for both of these hearts should measure about 10cm (4in) across the base and be about 3cm (1¼in) high.

1 Roll thin sausages of dough and wind them into coil shapes. Attach to the flat surround of the heart with dough paste. Roll small balls of dough and position one between each coil. Indent each ball with the end of your paint brush. Attach coils and balls of dough all around the heart.

2. Half-bake the heart. When the dough is firm enough to handle, remove the foil mould and return to the oven to finish baking. (For more .information on baking see pages 17–18.) Allow it to cool and apply a wash of purple paint (but not over the decorative balls and coils).

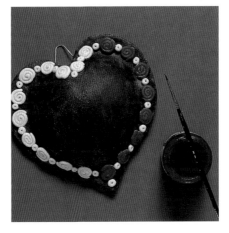

3 Paint the coils with red paint or with another contrasting colour.

4 Paint the balls with gold paint. Highlight the coils by dabbing a tiny amount of gold paint over each one. When the paint is dry, varnish.

TO MAKE THE SWIRLED HEART

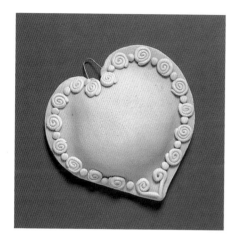

MATERIALS AND EQUIPMENT

Salt dough (see page 12)
Dough paste (see page 13)
Non-stick baking sheet
Ruler
Rolling pin
Heart template (page 137)
Small kitchen knife
Small wooden spatula
Aluminium foil
Brushes for applying dough paste, paints
and varnish
Pastry brush
Fish slice
1mm-thick wire, about 7cm (2¾in) for
each hanging loop
Wire cutters
Round-ended pliers
Rag or paper towel to apply paint finishes
Water-based paints
Gloss polyurethane varnish

1 Make coils as in step 1 opposite. Attach coils around the edge of the heart with a small flattened ball of dough in between each coil. Attach with dough paste. To make the detail at the lower point, roll two coils and leave a tail of dough trailing from each. Position them as in the photograph.

2 Half-bake the heart. When the dough is firm enough to handle, remove the foil mould and return to the oven to finish baking (see pages 17–18). Allow to cool. Paint a wash of pink over the heart (leaving the decorated edge of the heart unpainted).

3 Paint the coils, balls and the edge of the heart in black. Next paint a swirl pattern over the middle of the heart. Allow to dry.

4 Dab gold paint over the coils, balls and edge. Before the gold paint is completely dry, rub with a soft rag to expose patches of black. Highlight some of the swirls with dashes of gold paint. When the paint is dry, varnish your heart.

TO MAKE THE CUT-OUT HEART

For the Cut-out and Cupid's Arrow Hearts follow steps 1–2 of Heart of Gold (see page 104). For both of these hearts, the foil dome should measure about 10cm (4in) across the base and be about 3cm (1¼in) high.

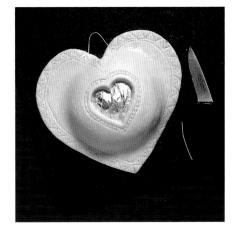

1 Cut out the inner heart with the small heart template or a pastry cutter. Apply enough pressure to cut through the dough, but avoid pressing into the foil mould. When you have made your heart-shaped cut-out, smooth the inner edges. If the main heart shape has become at all distorted, gently push it back into shape.

2 Score two lines, about 4mm (¼in) apart, around the inner heart. Make small indentations between one set of lines. Score two lines (about 3mm (⅛in) apart) and about 1cm (⅜in) in from the outer edge of the heart. Now score a zigzag pattern around the outside. Make indentations between the triangle shapes formed by the zigzags.

3 Half-bake the heart, remove the foil mould and return to the oven to finish baking. When cool, paint the main body of the heart gold. Leave the scored lines and indentations unpainted.

4 Now paint the triangles (created by the zigzag scoring) around the outer edge. These look dramatic painted black or choose another dark, contrasting colour. When the paint is dry, varnish your heart.

TO MAKE THE CUPID'S ARROW HEART

MATERIALS AND EQUIPMENT

Salt dough (see page 12)
Dough paste (see page 13)
Non-stick baking sheet
Ruler
Rolling pin
Heart templates (pages 136 and 137)
Small kitchen knife
Small wooden spatula
Aluminium foil
Brushes for applying dough paste, paints
and varnish
Pastry brush
Fish slice
1mm-thick wire, about 7cm (2¾in) for each
hanging loop, and 51cm (20in) for the arrow
Wire cutters
Round-ended pliers
Rag or paper towel to apply paint finishes
Water-based paints
Gloss polyurethane varnish

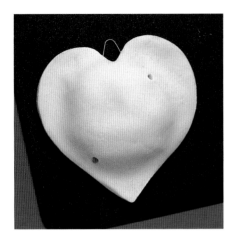

1 Make the holes for your wire arrow. Do this by pushing a the end of a paint brush through the raised part of the dough. Make one hole at a time – the first in the top right-hand side of the heart and the second in the lower left-hand side. Pierce the dough sideways on, pushing your paint brush through at an angle.

2 Half-bake the heart, remove the foil mould and return to the oven to finish baking (see pages 17–18). For the arrow, cut about 51cm (20in) of wire. Fold it in half and twist loosely once or twice. Using pliers, bend the wire about 10cm (4in) up from the ends and separate into two lengths. Coil the end of each length.

3 When the dough heart is baked, take it from the oven and let it cool. Give the heart a solid base coat of red paint.

4 Dab on a mottled highlight effect with a soft rag dipped in gold paint. When the paint is dry, varnish the heart. Allow the varnish to dry thoroughly. Finally, thread the wire arrow through the heart.

ROLLED HEART WITH ROSES

This heart involves no templates or patterns – the whole project is modelled by hand, which makes it very easy to vary its size and thickness. The heart itself is simply a hand-rolled "sausage" which is curved into shape and then secured with dough paste. To make a smaller heart, just roll a shorter, slimmer sausage, or roll a longer, thicker piece to make a larger version of the same design.

Two hand-modelled roses are a pretty addition, but if you prefer a more elaborate finish, you could cover the whole surface with leaves and flowers. Add a larger hanging loop to support heavier designs. Finally, thread your heart with beads and a bell (adding more beads to a longer piece of wire if your heart is bigger than the one featured here).

MATERIALS AND EQUIPMENT

Salt dough (see page 12)
Dough paste (see page 13)
Non-stick baking sheet
Ruler
Rolling pin
Small kitchen knife
Small wooden spatula
Brushes for applying dough paste, paints
and varnish
Pastry brush
1mm-thick wire, about 13cm (5in)
Wire cutters
Round-ended pliers
Beads and bell
Water-based paints
Gloss polyurethane varnish

1 Roll a dough sausage, about 25cm (10in) long and 2cm (³/₄in) thick and curve it into a heart shape. Make a hanging loop with about 7cm (2³/₄in) of wire (see page 16), embed it into the heart. Cut a piece of wire, about 6cm (2³/₈in), and bend a loop at one end. Push down through the heart leaving about 3cm (1¹/₄in) hanging down.

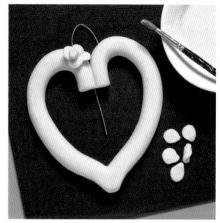

2 To make the roses, flatten a small ball of dough between your thumb and forefinger. Roll this petal into an upside-down cone shape that will form the centre of the rose. Make four more petals and attach them to the bottom of the cone shape with a little dough paste. Attach a rose to each side of the heart with dough paste.

3 To make leaves, roll out dough to a thickness of about 2mm (¹/₈in). Cut out four leaf shapes. Neaten any rough edges. Score a line down the centre of each leaf. Score vein lines on either side of the central line. Attach with dough paste. (Each pair of leaves should overlap slightly.)

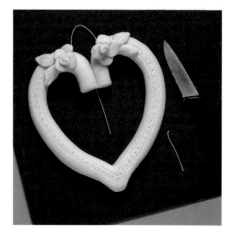

4 Add decoration to the heart shape by scoring two lines (about 5mm (¹/₄in) apart) along the surface. Using the end of a paint brush or the point of a knife, make a row of indentations inside the lines. Bake the heart (see pages 17–18 for more information on baking).

5 When cool, paint, using the photograph as a guide. Allow to dry and then varnish. Thread the beads and the bell onto the wire in the middle. Finally, bend a loop into the end of the wire to lock the threaded decorations in place.

1 Roll out dough to a thickness of about 1cm (⅜in). Working straight onto the baking sheet, cut around the base template and the small heart shape, with a sharp knife. Smooth and neaten any rough edges with a spatula or damp paint brush.

DOVE PLAQUE

This dove plaque is a very symbolic way to mark an engagement or anniversary. If you paint in the names of the couple involved, the plaque becomes even more personal – or add the date to make a lasting record of the happy event.

Templates are provided to help you cut the dough shapes to exactly the right size. Laying dough pieces on a flat base is a very effective way of bringing a design to life, but only if the relief-work is an even thickness. For a neat finish, roll your dough out carefully, and smooth any rough edges before laying relief shapes on the plaque base. Try not to distort the dough and make sure that scored lines and indentations are evenly applied, to an equal depth.

2 Using the point of your knife and a ruler, score three lines, about 3mm (⅛in) apart, across the plaque underneath the heart. Score a single line about 1.5cm (⅝in) up from the bottom edge of the plaque, curving the line as you go, and two short vertical lines in the middle. With the wire, make a hanging loop (see page 16). Embed the loop in the top of the plaque.

MATERIALS AND EQUIPMENT
Salt dough (see page 12)
Dough paste (see page 13)
Non-stick baking sheet
Ruler
Rolling pin
Templates (page 139)
Small kitchen knife
Small wooden spatula
Brushes for applying dough paste, paints and varnish
Pastry brush
Fish slice
1mm-thick wire, about 7cm (2¾in)
Wire cutters
Round-ended pliers
Rag or paper towel to apply paint finishes
Water-based paints
Gloss polyurethane varnish

3 Roll out more dough, this time, to a thickness of about 5mm (¼in). Cut around the two dove templates. Smooth and tidy any rough edges.

4 Carefully lift the larger dove shape and place it on the dough plaque. Attach with dough paste. Make sure that the bottom edge of the dove shape is in line with (and touches) the curved scored in line. The dove's wings should jut out beyond the edges of the plaque.

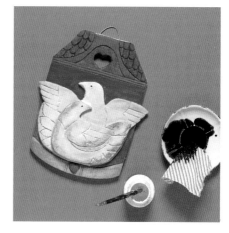

5 Lay the second dove shape on top of the first and attach with dough paste. Smooth and tidy any rough edges with a spatula. With the end of a small paint brush or the point of a knife, make an eye indentation in both dove shapes. Follow the photograph to score in the feathers and wings.

6 Cut out a tiny heart and place at the bottom of the plaque. Now score in the roof detail. The tiles on either side of the roof shape must be clearly defined, so score slightly thicker lines (by using a wider knife-point, or by going over the same line twice). Take care not to cut too deep. Bake and brown off your plaque (see pages 17–18 for more information).

7 When cool, paint the plaque. Use bright, toning colours for the background, tiny heart and roof (don't paint the space below the dove shapes). Paint the doves white or cream. When the paint is almost dry, highlight the wing-tips, the necks and the ends of the feathers by dabbing on a tiny amount of black paint with a soft rag or the tip of your forefinger. Varnish.

WEDDING PLAQUE

Decorative plaques with a personal theme make wonderful gifts – especially when they are given to commemorate a once-in-a-lifetime occasion. This wedding plaque is actually very easy to assemble. When the template shapes have been cut, place them on an evenly rolled area of raw dough and cut around them carefully. It is important to smooth and blend the relief work to a neat finish, so take your time. Small details and decorative paint effects give this plaque a special appeal. Balls of dough, squeezed through a garlic press are used to trim the bride's dress and veil and a wash of gold over a white paint base adds a luxurious, shimmering finish to her wedding outfit.

MATERIALS AND EQUIPMENT

Salt dough (see page 12)

Dough paste (see page 13)

Non-stick baking sheet

Ruler

Rolling pin

Templates (page 138)

Small kitchen knife

Small wooden spatula

Garlic press

Brushes for applying dough paste, paints
and varnish

Pastry brush

Fish slice

1mm-thick wire, about 7cm (2¾in)

Wire cutters

Round-ended pliers

Rag or paper towel to apply paint finishes

Water-based paints

Gloss polyurethane varnish

1 Working straight onto the baking sheet, roll out dough to an even thickness of 5mm (¼in). Put your template on the dough and cut around it to make the base shape of the plaque. Smooth all rough edges and correct any distortion in shape. Make a heart-shaped hanging loop from the 7cm (2¾in) length of wire (see page 16) and embed it in the top of the plaque.

2 Roll out more dough to a thickness of 3mm (⅛in). Cut around templates to make the bride's veil, the groom's jacket and the bride and groom's faces. The dough is very thin, so use a fish slice to transfer the shapes to the base shape. Position the shapes (faces first) according to the photograph and attach with dough paste. Make sure that all edges are smooth (fill any gaps with thickened dough paste).

3 Roll two sausages, each about 5cm (2in) long and about 1cm (⅜in) wide. Squeeze the ends into points. Using the photograph as a guide, position the arms and attach with dough paste. Blend the edges of the arms into the base shape. Score in a dividing line between the bride and groom's faces and lower bodies. Score more lines (three) across the bride and groom's ankles.

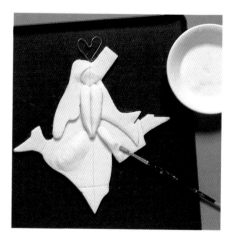

4 To create slight relief, roll two dough sausages. Place one dough sausage on the skirt and one on the trousers and blend these shapes into the base shape.

5 Roll another sausage to make the brim of the groom's hat. Roll two small dough balls, attach them to the bride and groom's faces and shape them into noses. The groom's moustache is two small sausages of dough with pointed ends. Score in the shoe laces, heels and trouser stripes.

6 Roll a sausage of dough for the groom's cuff. Make the trim for the bride's dress and veil by squeezing dough through a garlic press. Drape some strands on the cuff and along edges of the veil, attach with dough paste. Bake (see pages 17–18). Paint, using the photograph as a guide.

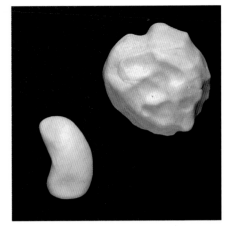

1 Working straight onto the baking sheet, roll a fat sausage of dough, about 7cm (2³⁄₄in) long and about 2.5cm (1in) thick. Using the photograph as a guide, model the sausage into a body shape. Make sure that the back of the dough is flat.

PAPERWEIGHTS

These paperweights are designed to make the most of the rich golden-brown of baked dough. Touches of black and/or white add contrast to hats (or hair) and the vivid scarlet of a clutched heart can be glimpsed inside each figure's grasp. Modelled entirely by hand, the paperweights' rounded contours and smooth surfaces are pro-duced by blending the raw dough into a series of neat curves. The instructions show how to make the figure with the pointed hat. For the other two paper-weights, follow the same instructions, but model a wide-brimmed hat and squeeze the edge into a wavy brim for one figure, and make hair from small rolls of dough for the other.

MATERIALS AND EQUIPMENT
Salt dough (see page 12)
Dough paste (see page 13)
Non-stick baking sheet
Ruler
Small kitchen knife
Small wooden spatula
Brushes for applying dough paste, paints and varnish
Water-based paints
Gloss polyurethane varnish

 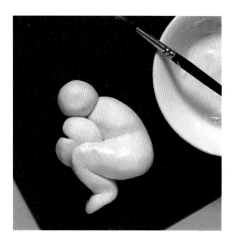 

2 Roll a ball for the head about 2cm (³⁄₄in) long and about 2cm (³⁄₄in) thick. Attach the head to the body by applying dough paste and pressing gently into position. Make the heart by rolling a ball of dough, flattening the back and indenting the top with the blunt edge of a knife. Attach the heart with dough paste and press gently in position.

3 To make the thigh, roll a thick sausage of dough about 7cm (2³⁄₄in) long 2cm (³⁄₄in) thick. Make the top of the thigh rounder and thicker than the lower part. Attach with dough paste. Roll a sausage of dough, about 8cm (3in) long and 2cm (³⁄₄in) thick, and shape into a leg and foot and attach with dough paste. Make sure that the back of the dough is flat.

4 Roll a slightly thinner sausage of dough for the arm, long enough to lay across the body and heart. Position this piece and attach it with a little dough paste. The hat is simply a ball of dough, flattened at the base and pulled into a point at the top. Mould the hat into position on top of the head (using a little dough paste to attach it). The back of the hat should be flat. Score lines across the dough with the blade of a knife.

5 Attach a tiny ball of dough for the ear. Then attach a small ball of dough for the nose, carefully blending it into shape. The eye sockets are shallow indentations, made with the end of a paint brush. Bake the dough figure, turn the oven to a higher setting and brown off until it takes on the smooth brown shades of rich skin-tones. (For more information on baking see pages 17–18.) When cool, paint in the stripes and spots on the hat and paint the heart red. Wait for the paint to dry thoroughly before varnishing.

PARTY PIECES

Fantasy animals make perfect favours for children's parties. Quick and easy to produce, the technique couldn't be simpler. Just cut out their shapes, using the templates provided and use your imagination to transform the cut-outs into entirely original salt-dough gifts for each of your guests. When it comes to paint finishes, anything goes – either ignore realism entirely and choose bright colours and crazy patterns for maximum impact, or opt for something more subtle.

Either leave the shapes as they are or (after painting and varnishing) make them into badges by sticking safety clasps to their backs. These projects are designed to be adapted, so you don't have to use our printed templates. Make freehand shapes by cutting straight into the dough with a sharp knife, or use pastry cutters and even children's craft cutters to stamp out alternative designs.

Napkin rings have instant appeal because as well as being practical, they add originality and interest to a festive table. Use them as table decorations and then present them to your guests when the celebration ends.

The instructions show you how to make a pig napkin ring. The other animal napkin rings use exactly the same cut-out technique, but vary in shape and surface pattern. (You will find templates on page 140.)

When you come to decorate your napkin rings, either paint them to blend in with other table decorations, or make them stand out by using rich, contrasting colours. For more information on painting see pages 19–20.

TO MAKE THE PIG NAPKIN RING

MATERIALS AND EQUIPMENT
Salt dough (see page 12)
Dough paste (see page 13)
Non-stick baking sheet
Rolling pin
Pig napkin ring template (page 140)
Small kitchen knife
Small wooden spatula
*Brushes for applying dough paste, paints
and varnish*
Rag or paper towel to apply paint finishes
Water-based paints
Gloss polyurethane varnish

1 Roll dough to a thickness of 1.5cm (⅝in). Place the pig template on top of the dough and using a small kitchen knife, cut around the cardboard shape. Smooth any rough edges. Adjust any distortion in shape by patting gently with the flat edge of your knife or with a small spatula.

2 To make the pig's tail, roll a small piece of dough and bend it into a coil shape. Attach the tail to the pig using a little dough paste.

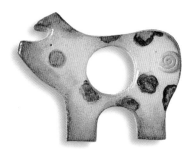

3 Bake the napkin ring, brown off and allow to cool. (For more information on baking see pages 17–18.)

4 Add spot details by dipping your finger into a small amount of black paint and dabbing it on. Do the same for the cheek (with a little red paint). When the paint is dry, varnish.

Home-made napkin rings and party favours make charming additions to any party table. The simple bird shape, above, was cut out from a template on page 140 and baked with the other animal rings featured on these pages. A rich base shade provides a contrasting background for a delicate gold pattern, applied with a fine-bristled brush, and layers of high-gloss varnish produce a lustrous sheen.

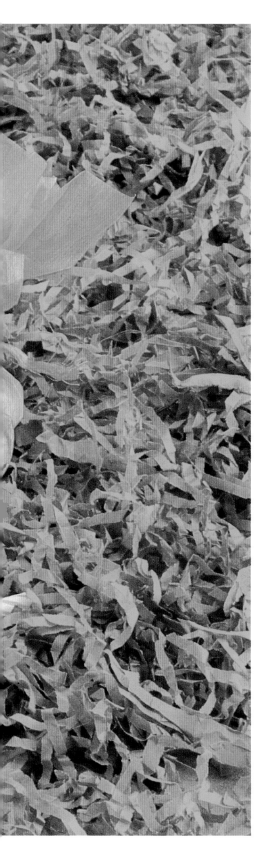

PIGLET HOUSE

A thatched cottage, hiding three nursery-rhyme piglets is bound to appeal to anyone with a taste for surprises. This project makes a delightful table decoration for parties and celebrations, particularly if children are involved. Model extra piglets as party favours (one for each guest), or fill the house with sweets and small gifts.

The house is simply moulded over cardboard and decorated with fine strands of dough and surface scoring. Working with a three-dimensional shape is not difficult, but don't press too hard (particularly when scoring), in case you distort the dough. Transform the flat dough base into a colourful garden by applying a generous wash of green paint and then decorate your flower border in bright, cheerful shades.

When you varnish your model, use a thicker brush for the house and garden and a fine-bristled brush for the piglets. Small amounts of varnish, applied in thin, even layers produce the smoothest finish. Make sure that each coat is completely dry before applying the next, and clean your brushes thoroughly between applications.

MATERIALS AND EQUIPMENT

Salt dough (see page 12)
Dough paste (see page 13)
Non-stick baking sheet
Ruler
Rolling pin
Templates (page 141)
Small kitchen knife
Small wooden spatula
Aluminium foil
Garlic press
Brushes for applying dough paste, paints
and varnish
Rag or paper towel to apply paint finishes
Water-based paints
Gloss polyurethane varnish

1 Using the cardboard template, make up the triangular mould for the piglet house. Secure tabs with sticky tape. Carefully cover the cardboard with aluminium foil (take your time over this – the card must be covered entirely). Now smooth the foil to give a good, flat moulding surface.

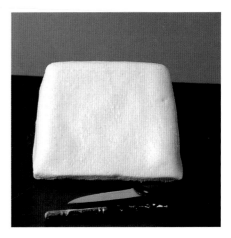

2 Roll out dough to a thickness of 5mm (¼in) and carefully cover the mould. Trim off any excess dough. Smooth the surface and neaten rough edges.

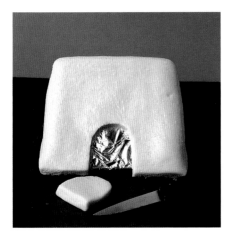

3 Cut a door-shape out of the dough. Take care not to cut into the foil-covered mould underneath. Smooth rough edges and alter any overall distortion in shape.

4 Using a small kitchen knife, score all over the surface of the house. Working on one side of the house at a time, score in straight, vertical lines followed by diagonal lines.

5 Squeeze balls of dough through a garlic press to make strands, about 5cm (2in) long, for the roof. Use dough paste to attach the strands along the top of the house. Gently squeeze a clump of strands into a chimney shape and attach to the roof with dough paste. Arrange a few dough strands around the front door and attach them with dough paste.

6 Roll out more dough to a thickness of 5mm (¼in). Lay the base template on top of the dough and cut around it. Smooth any rough surfaces. Push balls of dough through a garlic press. Laying down two or three strands at a time, make a narrow flower border around the base. Attach the strands to the base with dough paste.

7 Roll balls of dough by hand. Attach them to the border with dough paste. Using the end of a paint brush, indent the centre of each ball. Now make petal shapes by scoring lines around the indentation. Model tiny leaves by flattening small balls of dough between your thumb and forefinger. Attach them to the border.

8 To make a piglet, roll two balls of dough, one slightly larger than the other. Stick them together with a little dough paste. Now attach a tiny ball for the nose, and indent it twice to make nostrils. Roll two tiny sausage shapes for ears and attach them with dough paste. The legs are simply four small sausage shapes. Attach them with dough paste. Score in the hooves. Roll a thin sausage and coil it into a tail. Attach the tail to the piglet with dough paste. Repeat to make more pigs.

9 Bake the base, the house and the piglets. (Remember that smaller items will be ready sooner than larger pieces – see pages 17–18 for more information on baking). When the pieces are cool, use the photograph as a guide for your paintwork. When the paint is dry, varnish each part carefully.

MATERIALS AND EQUIPMENT

Salt dough (see page 12)
Dough paste (see page 13)
Non-stick baking sheet
Ruler
Small kitchen knife
Small wooden spatula
1mm-thick wire, about 7cm (2³/₄in)
Small piece of aluminium foil
Wire cutters
Round-ended pliers
Brushes for applying dough paste, paints
and varnish
Rag or paper towel to apply paint finishes
Water-based paints
Gloss polyurethane varnish

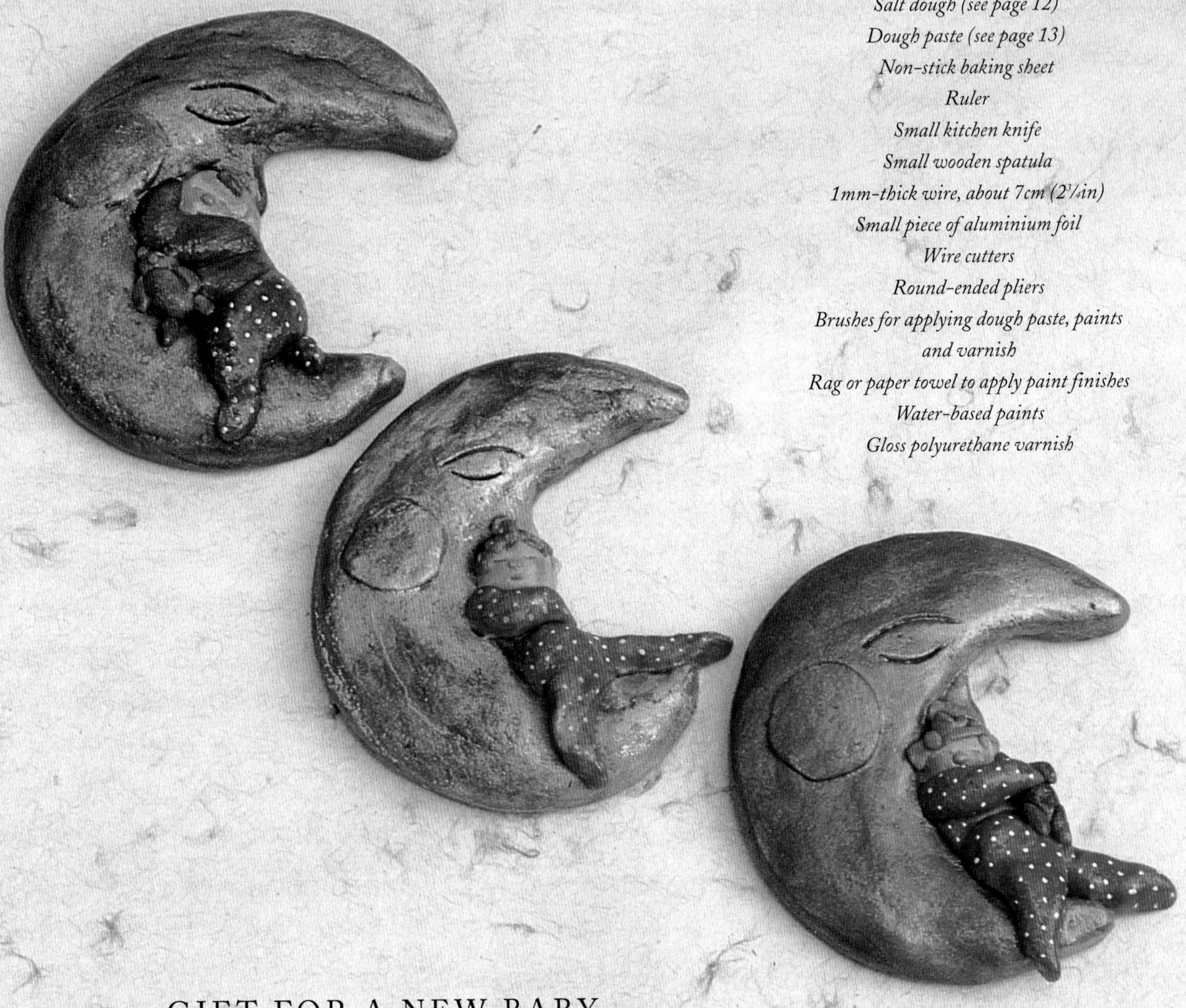

GIFT FOR A NEW BABY

This sleeping infant, cradled by a silver-blue moon, makes a charming gift for a new baby.

Although modelling this project by hand is not difficult, it is best to take your time. Allow the step-by-step photographs and instructions to guide you, and try to keep the baby in proportion to the moon's size.

If you want to add something personal for the child you have in mind, make a teddy bear or a favourite toy for the salt-dough baby to cuddle. Paint washes give the moon a mysterious, shimmering glow, but when you come to paint the baby, use stronger colours as a contrast, and apply details (like the patterned sleep-suit) with a fine brush.

1 Working straight onto the baking sheet, roll a very thick sausage of dough, about 30cm (12in) long and about 6cm (2⅜in) wide. Use the palm of your hand to squash and widen the dough, and your fingers to tease the ends into points, making a moon shape.

2 Make a hanging loop from the wire (see page 16). Turn the moon shape over and embed the ends of the loop into the moon, about 2cm (¾in) up from the centre. Wedge a small, folded piece of foil behind the loop to prevent it becoming embedded in the dough. Now turn the moon shape over again and adjust any change of shape.

3 Roll a cone of dough for the nose and squash it into shape. Attach it to the moon with dough paste, smoothing and blending it so that no joins are visible. (Attach all the features with dough paste.) Roll a small ball of dough and flatten it into a wide circle. Attach this cheek-piece to the moon. Score in the moon's eye.

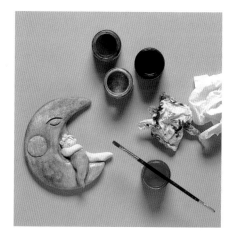

4 The baby's body is an oblong sausage. Roll this by hand and gently press it into place in the lower scoop of the moon shape. Roll a ball of dough for the baby's head. Attach it to the oblong body by pressing gently. Apply a little dough paste if necessary. (The baby's head should fit snugly under the moon's nose.)

5 Roll a sausage of dough for the arm and tease the end into a point. Position and attach. Make the legs by rolling two longer dough sausages. Tease the ends into points. Position and attach. The baby's ear and nose are tiny balls of dough. Attach them to the head shape. Score in the eyes and mouth. Make a bow from small sausages of dough. Position and attach.

6 Bake the plaque. (For information on baking, see pages 17–18.) When cool, paint the moon with washes of silver and blue. Dab on a little black paint and gently rub into the moon. Use brighter, contrasting colours for the baby's clothes and finish with tiny dots of white, applied with the point of a fine paint brush. When the paint is dry, varnish your plaque.

MAKING TEMPLATES

The template shapes provided on pages 130–141 relate to many of the projects in the book. The instructions for these projects include page numbers for the appropriate templates.

Templates are extremely straightforward to make. Try not to rush the tracing and cutting processes, though – good, clean, neat-edged shapes give better results and can be used time and time again.

Photocopying is a quick alternative to tracing. Simply cut out photocopies of the template shapes, lay them on a piece of cardboard and cut carefully around them.

MATERIALS

Cardboard – old cereal boxes are an ideal thickness, or buy sheets of card from stationers. Laminated card is more expensive, but tends to last longer and a wipe-clean surface is very useful when you are working with raw dough
Sharp pencil
Stanley knife, craft knife, scalpel or scissors
Tracing (or thin grease-proof) paper

1 Using a sharp pencil, trace shapes carefully onto tracing (or thin grease-proof) paper. Heavily shade over the outline.
2 Place the tracing on the cardboard face down and draw over the traced shape, pressing firmly enough to recreate the outline on the cardboard underneath.
3 Use a stanley knife, craft knife, scalpel or scissors to cut out the cardboard shapes.
4 Roll out the dough to the desired thickness, place the template on the dough and cut around it carefully.

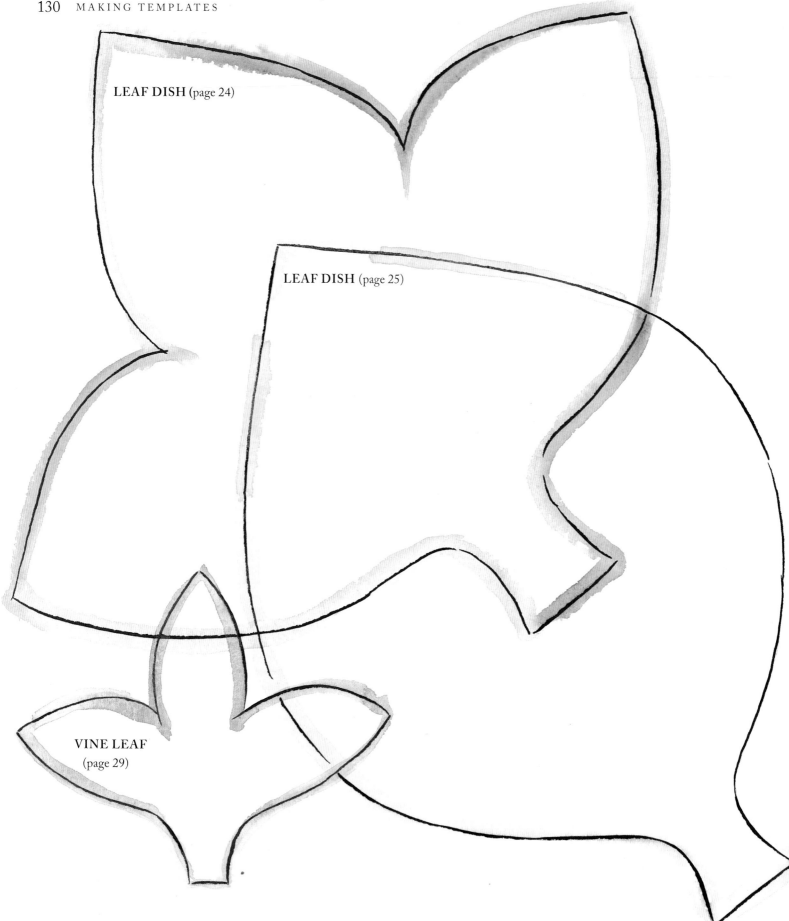

LEAF DISH (page 24)

LEAF DISH (page 25)

VINE LEAF
(page 29)

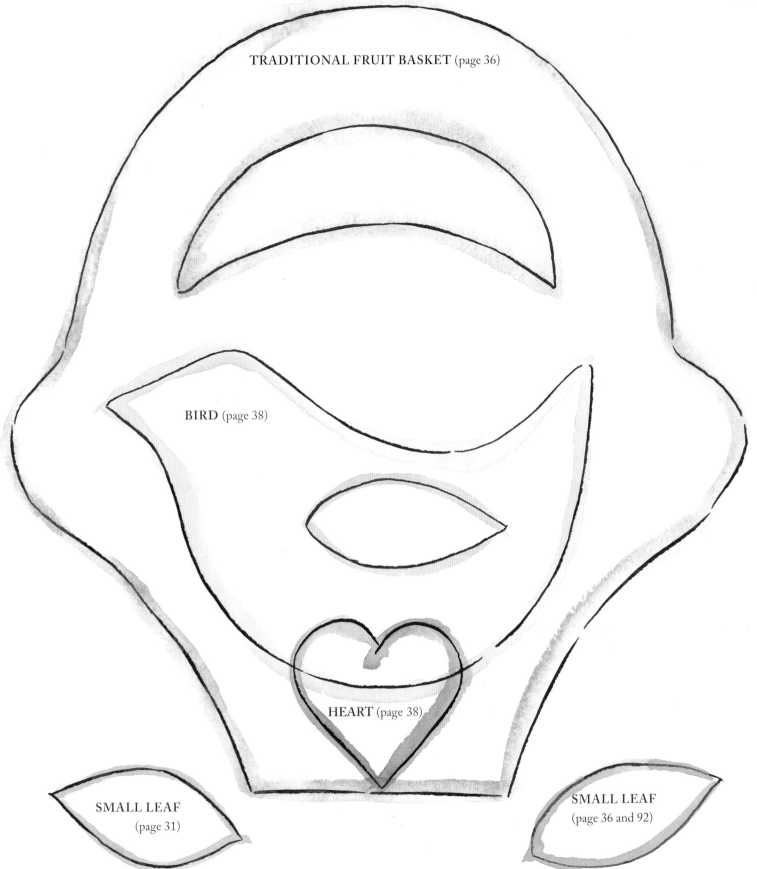

TRADITIONAL FRUIT BASKET (page 36)

BIRD (page 38)

HEART (page 38)

SMALL LEAF
(page 31)

SMALL LEAF
(page 36 and 92)

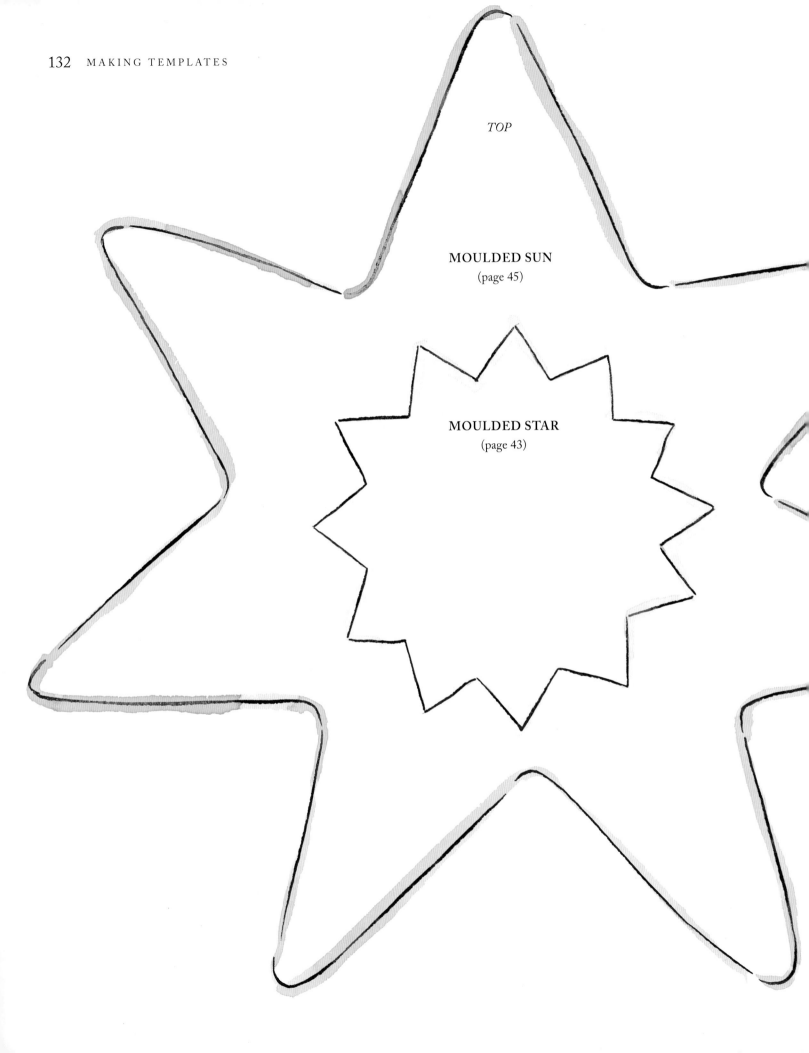

TOP

MOULDED SUN
(page 45)

MOULDED STAR
(page 43)

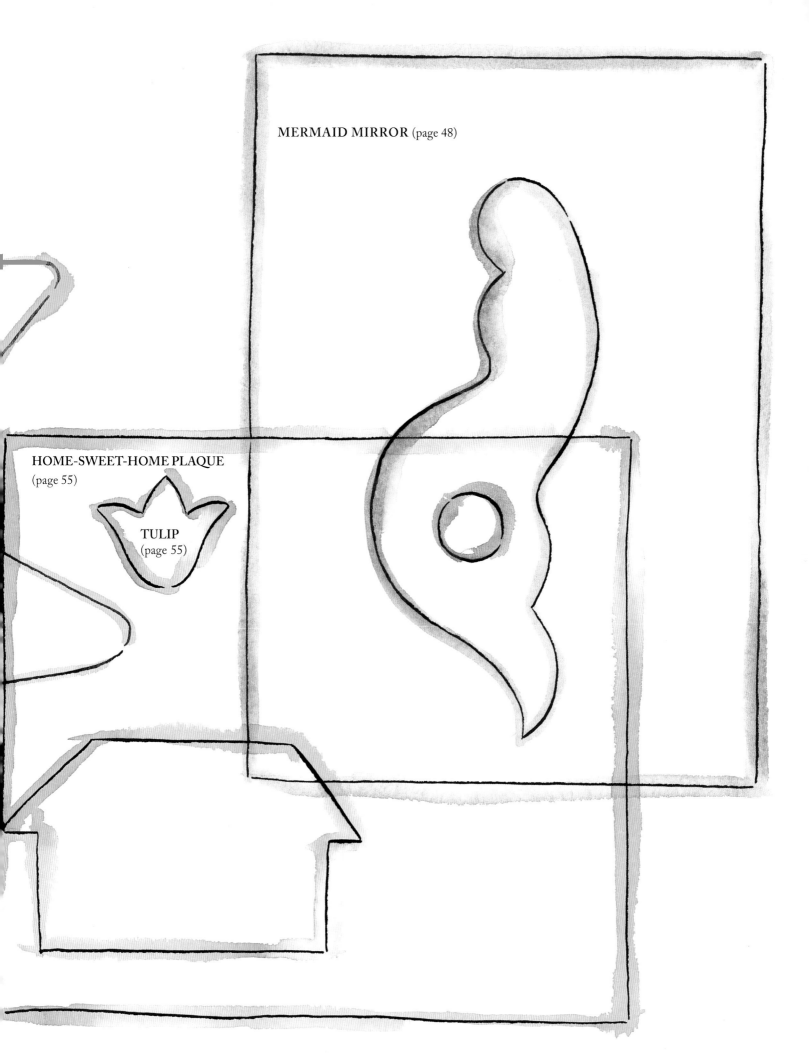

MERMAID MIRROR (page 48)

HOME-SWEET-HOME PLAQUE
(page 55)

TULIP
(page 55)

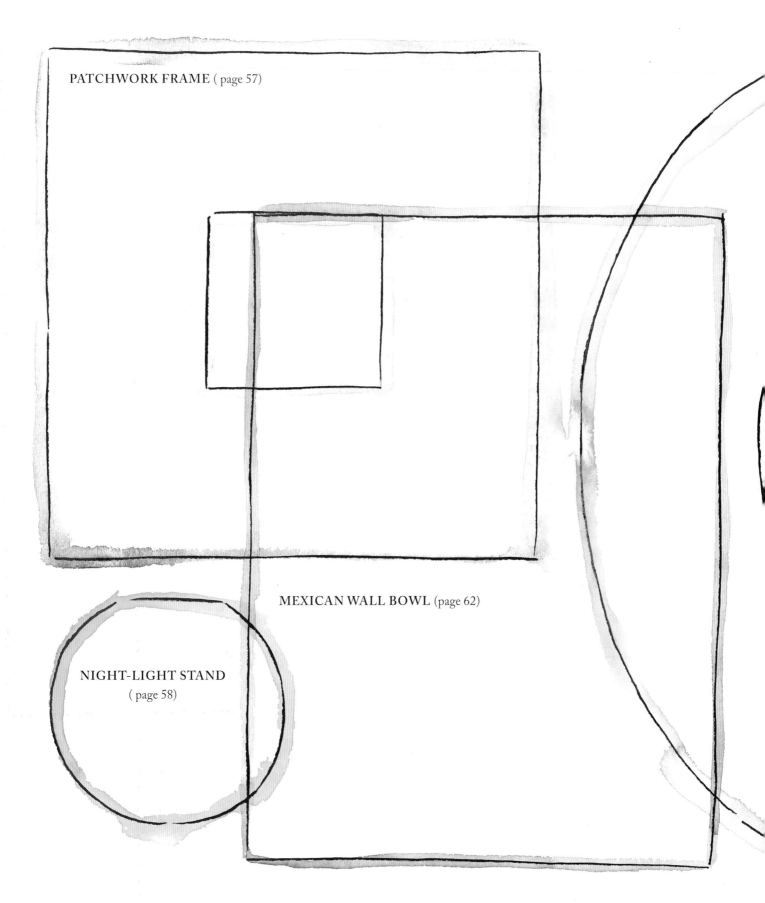

PATCHWORK FRAME (page 57)

MEXICAN WALL BOWL (page 62)

NIGHT-LIGHT STAND
(page 58)

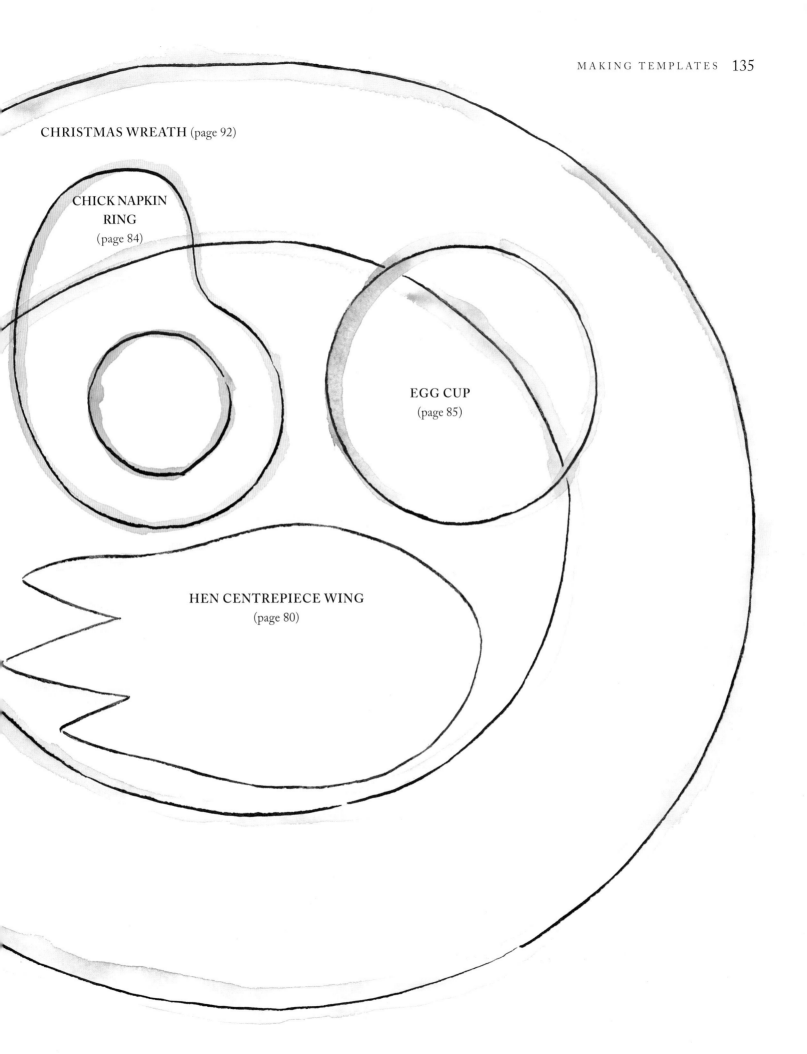

CHRISTMAS WREATH (page 92)

CHICK NAPKIN
RING
(page 84)

EGG CUP
(page 85)

HEN CENTREPIECE WING
(page 80)

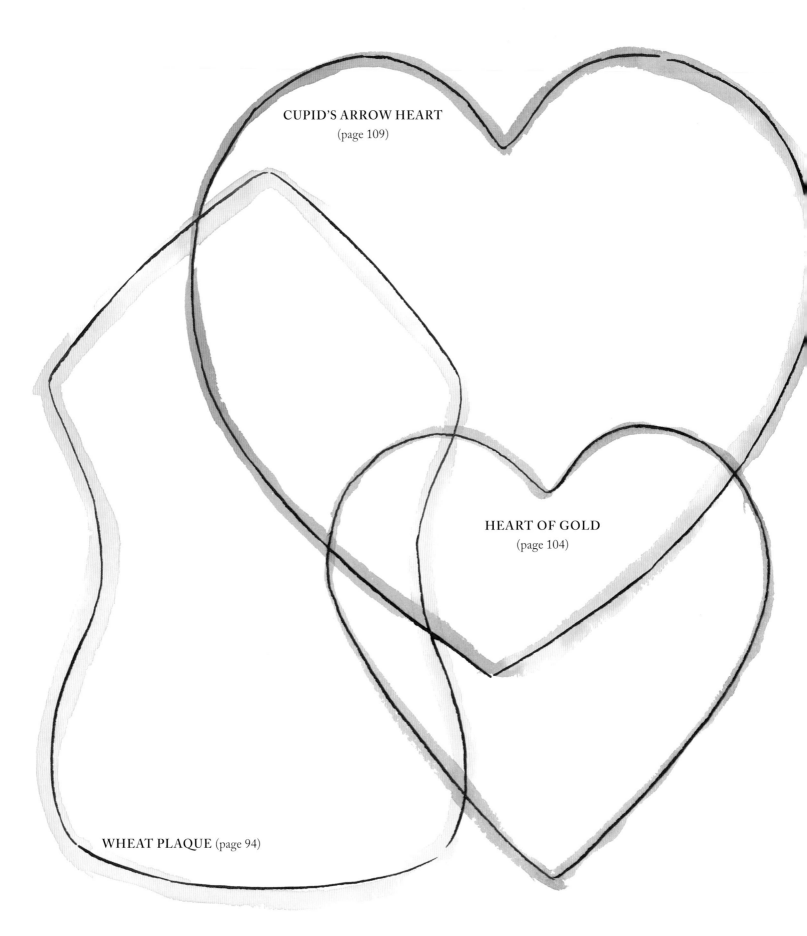

CUPID'S ARROW HEART
(page 109)

HEART OF GOLD
(page 104)

WHEAT PLAQUE (page 94)

CUT-OUT HEART
(page 108)

MOULDED, COILED AND
SWIRLED HEARTS
(pages 69, 106 and 107)

HEART FAVOUR
(page 118)

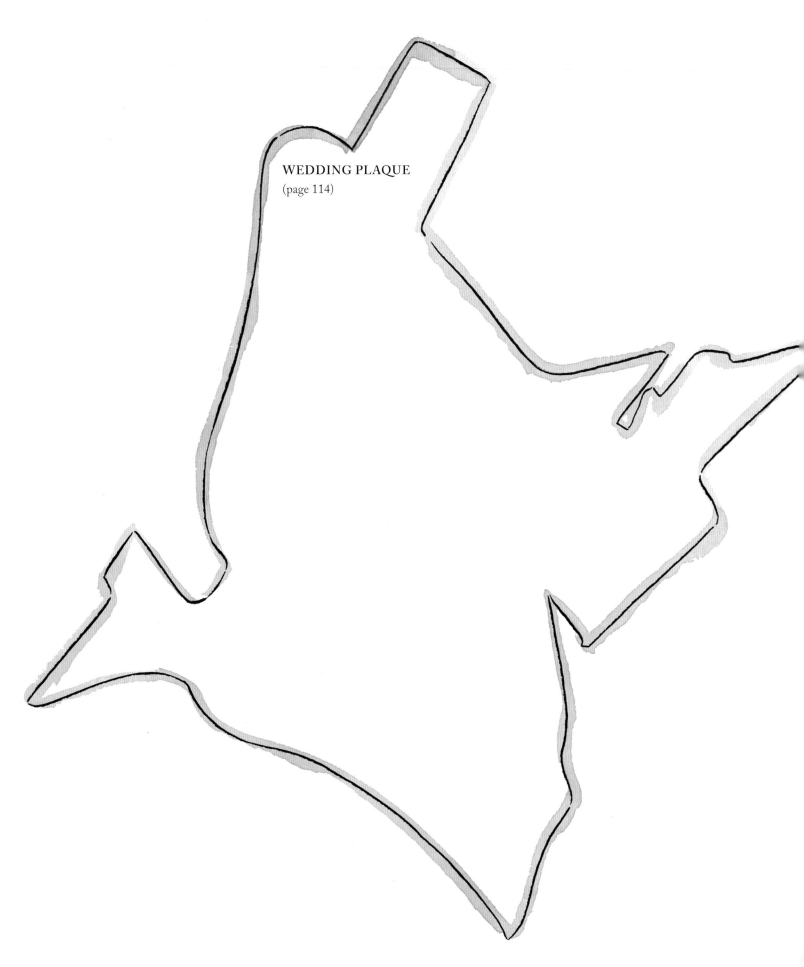

WEDDING PLAQUE
(page 114)

DOVE PLAQUE (page 113)

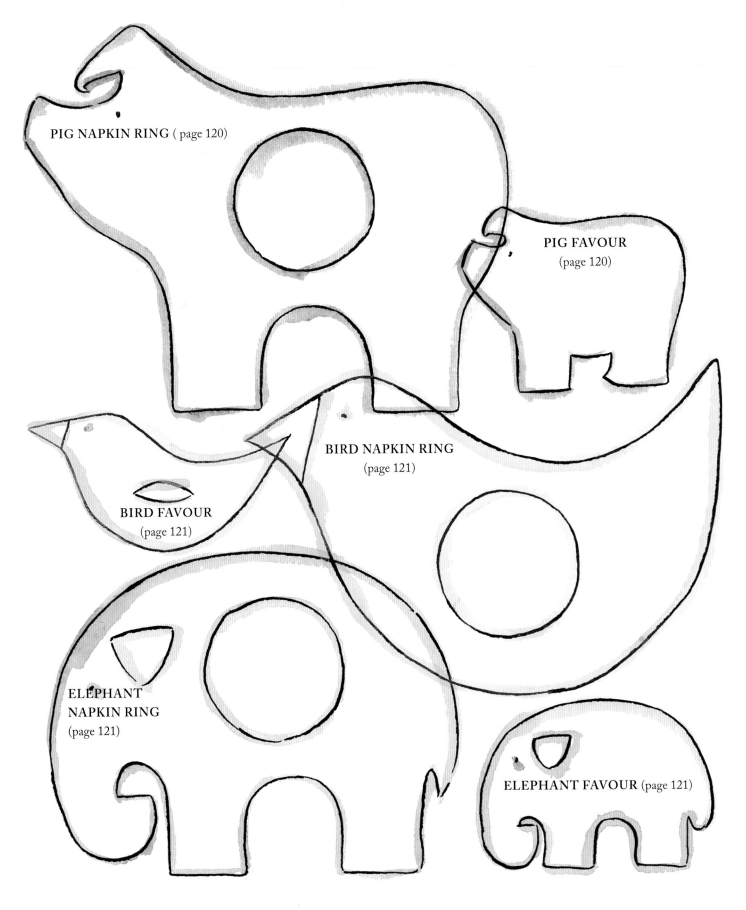

PIG NAPKIN RING (page 120)

PIG FAVOUR
(page 120)

BIRD NAPKIN RING
(page 121)

BIRD FAVOUR
(page 121)

ELEPHANT
NAPKIN RING
(page 121)

ELEPHANT FAVOUR (page 121)

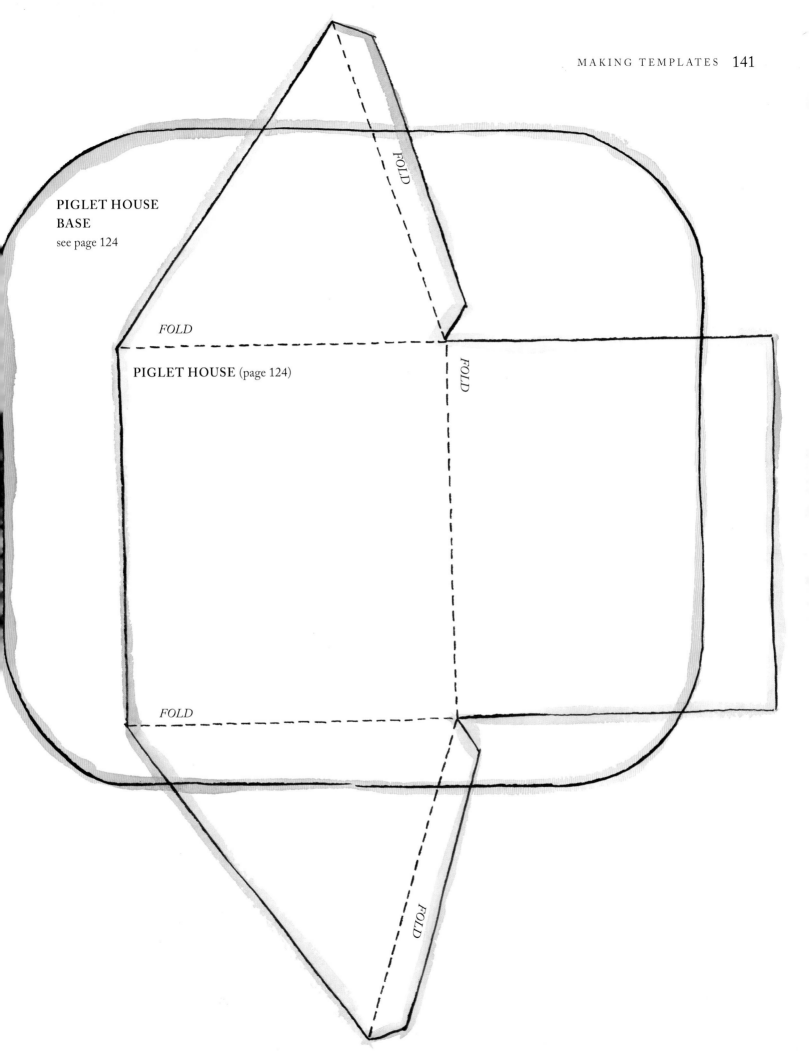

**PIGLET HOUSE
BASE**
see page 124

FOLD

PIGLET HOUSE (page 124)

FOLD

FOLD

FOLD

FOLD

INDEX

ACKNOWLEDGEMENTS

The publishers and authors would like to thank the following people
for their help and support in the production of this book:

Michael Hill for the template illustrations

Blake Minton for her help with the styling

Janine Tilley for her hospitality during the step-by-step photoshoot